From Pain to Purpose

Tammy Renee

From Pain to Purpose

Tammy Renee

Copyright © 2024 by Tammy Renee
From Pain to Purpose

All rights reserved.

Cover design by Leigh Bivens Publishing

Cover photograph by Calvin Finklea Photography

This self-published author supports the right to free expression and the value of copyright. The purpose of copyright is to encourage writers and artists to produce creative works that enrich our culture.

The scanning, uploading, and distributing of this book without permission is a theft of the author's intellectual property. Please contact the author if you would like permission to use material from the book (other than for review purposes). I appreciate your support of the author's rights.

Unless otherwise noted, scripture quotations are from the King James Bible Gateway online version.[1]

First edition: 2024

ISBN – 9798343764956

Printed in the United States of America

Library of Congress Control Number 2024913964

Dedication

First, to my Lord and Savior, Jesus Christ for his unwavering love and grace he is laid upon me.

To my mother and father, I want to express my gratitude for the unlimited love, support, and strength I drew from you during this period of my life.

To my beautiful daughter, my reason to keep moving, and to each of my family members and friends who encouraged me to write my story, I love and appreciate each and every one of you.

Acknowledgment

I give a big THANK YOU to all who contributed to my pain, hurt, and disappointments. You were an effective tool in pushing me "From Pain to Purpose."

Contents

INTRODUCTION 11

We are Here..14

Chapter 1 - Who Am I?..15

Growing Pains...17

A Bookmark...20

Discovering Who I Am..22

Chapter 2 - Life with Mom..25

Reunited..25

Babies R' Us..29

The Time I Escaped Death Row....................................30

Chapter 3 - There's No Place Like Home............................35

Getting My Education 39

The Church Life 39

The Servant's Heart 42

Signs & Wonders...44

Chapter 4 - Who Did I Marry?...47

Houston, We Have a Problem! 48

What a Girl Wants...55

What's Yours is Mine...60

And That's Mine Too!..65

Chapter 5 - Life Be Lifing - (Pt. 1) 69
    My Girl! 70
    Intruder Alert! 74
    You've Got What? 77
    Fight or Flight? 81
    The Benediction 85
    What the Devil Meant for Evil 86

Chapter 6 - Life Be Lifing - (Pt. 2) 89
    I Feel Like David 90
    Lifestyle Challenges 93
    Home-Sweet-Home 95

Chapter 7 - See What the Lord Has Done 103
    The Residue of Repeated Behavior 108
    What Happens in the War Room 111
    Purpose 113
    Beauty for Ashes 114
    Final Thoughts 117

About the Author 121

Introduction

As I start my first writing journey, I want to convey to all who read this book that I hope it inspires your hearts to place your faith and trust in our Almighty God. There is no one like Him.

While sitting in my office, thinking about the book, I didn't know what to say or even how to begin. I prayed and asked God to give me the words to encourage the hearts of His people. I told the Lord that I wanted to be a vessel to be used by Him in whatever capacity He desired.

God has been my unwavering friend, dependable Father, nurturing mother, steadfast lawyer, and reliable doctor. He is also my fervent lover, the greatest love of my life. When I close my eyes and reflect on my life's journey, I can vividly recall moments from age five, being aware of God and His power. He has consistently protected and shielded me as I matured physically and spiritually.

It can be and has been challenging to grow up without knowing my biological father. Evidently, my grandparents played a crucial role in providing me with love and support. Even though they were my support, I could not stop the yearning to uncover my genetic father's identity. I admit there was a deep desire for connection. This longing is a fundamental aspect of being human, even when the source of that connection is unknown.

Introduction

Likewise, I longed for a close relationship with my two sisters. We were biologically connected through our mom, but we didn't share fathers, which didn't matter to me. I just wanted to be someone's baby sister that was loved.

Over the years, I've become stronger in every aspect of my life, as I now better understand people and human nature. I've also become tough, but in a good way, and so I'm not made of nails; although I tried to put on a brave front as a teenager, when deep down, I spent many days shedding tears. Thoughts of my father consumed me. What did he look like? Did he stand tall, or was he of a short stature? Was he strong and muscular or slender? And where did he fall on the rich spectrum of Afrocentric shades? Whom did I resemble more, him or Mom? Unfortunately, all I had to hold onto was his name...

Then it happened, and life, as I knew it, changed. God saved me—hallelujah! He filled that void for me at 13 years old. Indeed, I didn't know much about Christ, but I knew I felt the love of God in my heart, and I knew I would never be the same again.

Reflecting on the incredible ways God has blessed my life, I am overwhelmed with gratitude, which warms my heart and brings tears of joy to my eyes. I feel compelled to share my testimony because I cannot imagine where I would be without God's presence. I am constantly thankful for His

Introduction

protection, which has shielded me from countless dangers and challenges.

In Psalms 91, we are told, **⁵Thou shalt not be afraid for the terror by night; nor for the arrow that flieth by day; ⁶ Nor for the pestilence that walketh in darkness; nor for the destruction that wasteth at noonday.**² This is God telling us that He will protect us from danger, seen and unseen, and He means that. How often have we been in unknown, dangerous situations that His grace sufficiently brought us through? He keeps us even when we don't know we need it, and sometimes when we don't want Him to (more about that later). At the end of the day, I found that God's grace and mercy were undeniable.

I thank God for pouring into me what needs to be shared so that it may touch the world and bring people to know Christ in the power of His blood and His resurrection.

I hold this book close to my heart because it represents a significant journey in my life. Through reflection, I am filled with gratitude towards God for His guidance and support during difficult times. I am thankful for the opportunity to be in this particular place and time, where I can share my story with others who may be encountering similar challenges as they, too, move from pain into purpose.

Introduction

We are Here

We were not brought into this world aimlessly; instead, we were created for a specific purpose. God intricately designed me with great plans in mind, and I believe He also has a unique plan and purpose for you. Throughout our lives, we are given various tasks and roles to fulfill, each serving a specific purpose in the season we find ourselves in. My deepest desire is to align my actions with God's intentions for my life.

I pray that you ask God for your purpose so that you can join His team in winning souls for Christ.

It's fascinating how many of us raised in a church environment or saved for a few years have heard countless Scriptures, yet our actions and beliefs often don't align. I'm not pointing fingers; I'm simply speaking from personal experience. But there are moments when we encounter difficult situations, and suddenly, a passage from the Scriptures takes on a new meaning. It completely transforms our connection with God.

It happened to me because I thought I knew God, but in this season of my life, I am experiencing Him differently, and I'm so grateful for that. Please pardon my preaching moment, but I get happy about sharing God's goodness! Therefore, as I dive deeper into my narrative, I pray it brings deliverance to someone, even if it is just one person.

Chapter 1

Who Am I?

My formative years were characterized by innocence and an insatiable curiosity, particularly during my upbringing in the serene town of Niagara Falls. Life in our town was uncomplicated, and material wealth was not something we had in excess. However, we were blessed with abundant love and warmth, first from my doting grandparents during the initial decade of my life and later from my devoted mother. Love filled every nook and cranny of our modest dwelling, creating a genuinely nurturing environment with what they had to offer.

For my first 12 years of life, I was an introvert; I felt I had no voice because I did not fit in. However, after my 13th birthday, something miraculous happened, and I became a lover of the great outdoors, a lively and adventurous spirit from morning until night. The open spaces filled me with a sense of liberation, almost as if they helped me inhale more deeply. The entire town was my playground, and I felt like a grown-up in training despite the fact I was a mere teenager.

On the other hand, I disliked Sundays primarily because everyone in the community assembled at the church. Attending church was something I vehemently avoided, mainly due to my grandmother's ominous warning that if I went, the Holy Ghost would "get me." The cryptic nature of her words left me perplexed and uneasy, ultimately leading to my decision to stay away from church.

I often felt like a misfit puzzle piece during my preteen years. I stood tall among my friends, but I was skinny, leading them to nickname me "Olive Oil" after the character from the Popeye cartoon. In contrast, my sisters Janice and Lisa were the embodiment of beauty, confidence, and popularity. They were widely known, whereas I seemed to blend into the background. This stark difference led me to grapple with my identity and struggle to fully accept and embrace myself for who I was.

I was that kid who always got picked on. They have since renamed it bullying. I was talked about badly; they called me bald head because I didn't have long hair like everyone else.

When I was a young child, hurtful words were spoken to me, which led to a negative mindset about myself. For example, someone said that my mom found me in a trash can because I didn't know who my father was. This caused me to grow up feeling unattractive with low self-esteem, and until I turned 13, I stayed close to home before becoming a tomboy.

The emotional struggle we experience is unfortunate when we don't know what the Word of God says about us. This is why training our children in the Word of the Lord is vital.

As you can see, man had his opinion of me, which was not all that great. I had yet to learn I was on God's mind before He created the Earth. Like you, I was made on purpose - for His purpose and no one else's. I was yet to discover that I was fearfully and wonderfully made.[3] I didn't know that God had plans for me - plans to prosper me, not harm me, and plans to give me hope and a future.[4]

Nope. I didn't know those things, which caused me considerable growing pains.

Growing Pains

My grandparents lived in a two-bedroom, one-bath apartment with me and my oldest sister, Janice. I slept with my Grandma Ruby[5] and Janice in the other bedroom, and my grandfather, Jim,[6] slept on the sofa.

We lived there for years; Jim was the only one working but came home every Thursday and gave my grandmother the check to pay bills and buy groceries. We didn't have much, but now I can see how God always blessed us to have more than enough.

I remember whenever I wanted something as a child, like a pair of roller skates, a bike, or a skateboard, my grandfather, a licensed plumber, would do odd jobs to earn money to buy me these things.

When I was around nine or ten years old, I often found myself feeling like the odd one among the neighborhood kids. It seemed like I was always too afraid to speak up for myself, and it felt like I had no voice when I was around them. This experience of exclusion and being shunned, which is now referred to as the "cancel culture," left me feeling hurt and isolated. It seemed like the other children didn't think I met their standards, making me withdraw and keep to myself.

During that time, instead of going outside to play, I chose to stay indoors under the care of my Grandma Ruby. She could see that I needed to be outside and socializing, but I couldn't bring myself to face the rejection I felt from the others.

"Baby, why don't you go outside and get some sun?" she would urge.

"No, ma'am, I'm good here in the house," I would say.

Who Am I?

This period of withdrawal had a significant impact on me, and it took time for me to regain my confidence and sense of belonging. I often felt as if life had no real purpose for me. I carried a deep sadness, a spirit of rejection and dejection within me, yet I kept it hidden from everyone. However, even in those tumultuous and uncertain moments of my childhood, deep down in that small place in my heart, I believed that God always had a clear and meaningful plan for my life.

As a child, I spent a substantial amount of time grappling with the concept of popularity, particularly regarding how some of my peers seemed to gain favor due to their clothing or the girls with long, pretty hair. I struggled to comprehend the connection between these superficial traits and one's social standing. What did that have to do with anything? Why was I so different? Why didn't I get long hair, or why could I not have been a little bit shorter? This left me feeling isolated and friendless while knowing that my sisters had a lot of friends.

Parents, please consistently encourage your children from the beginning, no matter whether they are talented or not or even what they look like. It's essential to continue to support and uplift your children and grandchildren through prayer and encouragement. As you provide their physical nourishment, don't forget their emotional and spiritual nutrients. You'll be glad that you did.

Although devoted, my grandparents were not psychologically equipped to give me that extra encouragement I needed. Like most people, they worked with what they were given. One constant thing they did was show us love.

A Bookmark

A bookmark is used to mark the place where you left off and will eventually return to when reading books. Now, as it pertains to books, it is a great idea, but not so much for the human psyche. Sometimes, there are mental bookmarks that identify a place where something positive happened, and these are good memories. On the other hand, there are mental bookmarks that identify a place where something negative occurred, and this is called trauma, which leaves a scar.

I received one of my first mental bookmarks in 1971 when I started kindergarten. The clothing I had was the best my grandparents could do for me. I had no idea that I looked poor. As a result, the other children judged me and chose not to sit with me; kids can be cruel. This incident was bookmarked in my memory, and it jump-started my feelings of insecurity, which created an emotional scar. Imagine being judged over something I had no control over.

Who Am I?

By the time I got to elementary school, I was bullied. I haven't thought about these things in decades. I believe in transparency, so I am sharing another bookmark.

I often found myself in situations where I felt I didn't have the advantage despite being tall. This led to even more instances of bullying at school. But that all stopped when I got home. The only creature I felt understood my heart other than Grandma Ruby was my dog, Count, who was given to us by a friend of Mom's who, by the way, had a knack for giving our pets weird names.

Count was the first don, followed by Drac and Ula. So, we had three dogs named Count Drac-Ula. Mom is funny that way.

When people visited and saw Count, they would all ask, "What's your dog's name?"

We would say, "Count."

In turn, they would start, "Is it one, two, three…?"

We'd break out in laughter, "No, his name is Count!"

To me, he was more than just a pet; he was a loyal friend who provided me with the love and acceptance I longed for. Count and I spent innumerable hours together, often playing outside. Our favorite activity was running through the field and enjoying the simple pleasure of rolling in the grass.

During that time, my sisters were distant. Janice was with her friends, and Lisa lived across the street with Aunt Lynn. I was not to be outdone; I found solace at home with my grandfather. He was a remarkable man known for his love of drink, yet he never faltered in his responsibilities. He took care of my grandmother, who was dedicated to caring for our home, and despite his daily intoxication, he never missed a day of work. In the evenings, my grandmother could be found at the bingo hall, indulging in her passion. Therefore, I was never alone. I had Grandma Ruby to keep me company during the day and Grandpa Jim at night, which was good enough for me.

Discovering Who I Am

I named this chapter "Who Am I?" because, at thirteen, I was clueless. But still on that quest for connection, trying to find my tribe, as they say nowadays. I remember with great clarity the feeling of exclusion that I experienced. There was a teen club known as Heather Hall where the young people hung out. Janice and Lisa regularly attended this spot. To my dismay, they would often take my younger cousin but never extended an invitation to me due to our grandmother's disapproval.

Who Am I?

As the Easter holiday drew near, I yearned to be part of their world. I mustered up the courage to plead with my grandmother to allow me to join my sisters at the club, and much to my surprise, she gave me permission.

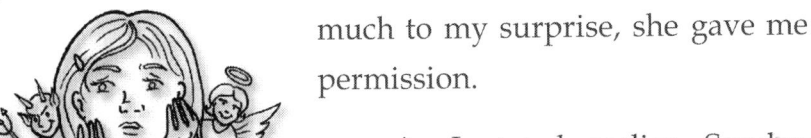

pixabay.com/vectors/angel-devil-female-guardian-human-1296384/

As I stated earlier, Sunday morning worship was not for me because of my fear of catching the Holy Ghost. However, I decided to go to church this Easter morning and called Aunt Lynn for a ride.

"Hello, Auntie, can I hitch a ride with you to attend church this morning?" I asked.

"Well, sure, Tammy, I'll be leaving in a few minutes."

Another mental bookmark took place soon after I walked into the church. The choir started their march down the aisle, and there she was in the front, a tall lady like me, wearing high heels. I was shocked that someone so tall would be brave enough to wear high heels, and she looked good, too! But there she was, standing like the Statue of Liberty in all of her glory, and at that moment, I felt a sense of belonging, a sense of acceptance for who I was. I felt connected. It was like I had looked in the mirror. I was validated. It was okay to be me. Hallelujah! I found Tammy. I know *who I am*!

From Pain to Purpose

The music filled the air, and I found myself loving the sound and feeling part of something bigger than myself. From that moment on, my life took a different path.

After the pastor finished preaching, I had a choice: Should I go out to the club that night or return to church? The decision was clear. I chose to return to church, and in that moment, the Lord started to work in me, guiding me on a journey of personal growth and self-discovery.

Chapter 2

LIFE WITH MOM

Right before the Lord started drawing me to Him, I remember He started with Momma. Let me say that she was not to be played with. When you stepped to her, you'd better step right! She had three girls to care for, and she had to keep us in line. I watched my sisters sometimes do what they wanted to despite being told "No." I would then watch Momma address their rebellion, which made me immediately straighten up.

Momma had come off the road from singing, took a job with Ford, and made preparations to bring her daughters home to live with her in Buffalo. I was unhappy about her decision. I didn't see that it was a fresh start for us. I could only see that it meant I would have to leave my school, grandmother, and friends. But at 12 years old, you don't have a vote in those matters, at least not back then. We did what we were told, so naturally, I was upset about moving as I packed my few belongings.

Reunited

My mom is a beautiful woman who was equally stunning in her youth. She was a recording artist back in the

'70s, which meant a lot of traveling. So, Janice and I lived with my grandparents, and Lisa lived with Aunt Lynn. Although she didn't live with us, we did see her daily.

I remember being told as a teenager that when my mother gave birth to me, she didn't want any more kids and left me in the hospital. Grandma Ruby sent Aunt Lynn to pick me up from the hospital, and I became Grandma's "Baby."

Long before this story was cleared up with my mother, I lived with a deep level of unspeakable pain and abandonment. I was separated from both of my parents, and well, it does something to my sense of self. My soul was damaged, and I felt torn up on the inside, like an old, discarded Rag Doll. But now, I'm so grateful to God for the "go-through" because it was worth it. We're told in the Word, *"When your father and your mother forsake you, then the Lord will take you up."*[7] Well, He was faithful to His word as He stood by me every step of the way, even after Momma and I were reunited in love.

From my understanding, when my mom gave birth to me, she was 21, and I was her fifth baby. However, only three of us are living due to Mom's miscarriage of the twins. I can't help but think how overwhelming it must have been for her. It was a different time for black people, and another mouth to feed was just too much. She is different now since she gave her life to Christ. We both have changed, and I love her with all my heart. I get it—the mindset, that is, now that I'm older.

I never asked Momma about the situation because we reconnected and bonded. Therefore, it no longer matters if there is truth to the story or not. All I know is that the woman who carried me for nine months and gave birth to me decided she wanted me back in her life, and this is where we will stay from this point on. I refuse to live my life burdened by a mother's wound.

For those who don't know, a mother's wound can create a sense of confusion and devastation in the child's mind and introduce deeply rooted beliefs that make the child feel unloved, emotionally abandoned, unworthy of care, and even fearful of expressing themselves. The wound can be so strong that it unconsciously affects their adult relationships and mental health. No thank you, I've met my quota. I didn't want that, so I forgave the past, and we have become best friends.

I praise God for loving me, cleansing my heart, and showing me how to love others. He mended my heart as only He could. Amen, and Hallelujah!

So, grudgingly, this twelve-year-old moved to Buffalo, another small town. Mom had a good job but was injured, which meant things got tight really quickly, and we had to depend on food stamps and welfare. I can remember it being so bad that Momma would chase rats early in the morning, and we could hear them in the attic, and yes, we had roaches, too.

It was horrible. When I think back, I didn't realize how poor we were in 1979. My mom was 33 years-old and had a 16, 14, and 12-year-old in her home. And then... Boom! A double portion of unexpected news came to our house. Lisa, who was 14, told Momma she was pregnant. A few days later, Janice, who was 16, echoed the same news. I know it's shocking to hear, but you can't make this stuff up. And by the time March of 1980 rolled around, we had two babies born two weeks apart in our home.

Because I was so young, I didn't understand what was going on. I didn't know or care where babies came from because my mind wasn't on those kinds of things. However, because of my sisters' decisions, Mom came for me. "Tammy, I'm putting you on the pill."

"No, Momma, I'm not going to have sex until I am married."

Little did I know I had prophesied over myself.

I didn't know who or why I was, and I couldn't quite figure out where I fit in. I was in Christ but had not yet learned I was supposed to be different, odd, and strange. It says so in 1 Peter 2:9, **"But ye are a chosen generation, a royal priesthood, a holy nation, a peculiar (strange, bizarre) people; that ye should shew forth the praises of Him who hath called you out of darkness into his marvelous light."**

And there it was, the explanation for Believers to hang on to when they have been made to feel different. We're supposed to!

Babies R' Us

Nine months later, our home was blessed with a beautiful niece from Lisa and a nephew from Janice. To me, they were playmates. But before they arrived, I had to deal with two grumpy pregnant sisters. It was not easy for me because they wanted nothing to do with me: no playing, no talking, no nothing. In my mind, they were being mean, but in hindsight, they were just pregnant teenagers who were probably very afraid for what their futures held.

Nevertheless, this was our first time with all three of us together, and I hoped to bond with them. But it didn't work out that way.

During that time, Janice was mean, but sometimes, she was my protector from Lisa. In hindsight, Lisa seemed extra mean because she had been separated from us. Earlier, I shared that she lived with Aunt Lynn while Momma sang on the road. Looking back, I can see how she must have felt a bit isolated, which caused her to be angry. But I hold no ill will about childhood misfortunes. I finally got the connection I so yearned for. I love both of my sisters, and we have become very close.

The Time I Escaped Death Row

My time in Buffalo was short-lived. I started school, and initially, I had no friends. Eventually, I met some people who were nice to me, but it wasn't the same as being back home in Niagara Falls with my friends.

Allow me a moment to share my rant about this move to Buffalo. First, I didn't want to go, and it wasn't that I didn't want to be with Momma—I did. But I was beginning to enjoy my friendships and feel good about myself. Second, I didn't want to move away from what I knew and where I was comfortable, so I began skipping school.

What happened was this: On my first day at school, the kids looked different and dressed well, which made me feel bad and ashamed. No one talked to me, and I dared not start a conversation. Slowly, it came from the shadows of my heart and mind, the bookmark from kindergarten where this same behavior hurt me before.

Walking down the hall toward my class, I overheard some girls talking about me. They were the "Mean Girls" who thought they were better than everyone else. So, when I entered the classroom to sit, they would look me up and down, giggle, and then force me out of the desk.

I was fully aware that my clothes didn't fit. I was extremely tall for my age, so we had to let the hem out of my pants and iron them to give me a bit more length, but I was still left in "high water" or "floods," as they were called. It's funny that Michael Jackson took this same look and was applauded for making it famous, but my pants invited a very different response.

Day after day, the torment became too much, and I once again retreated to that dark, emotional, antisocial cave, where I would eat lunch alone for a month. Some days, this place of being an outsider was more than I could stand. So, I came up with what I thought was a brilliant idea and decided not to return to school for about 12 weeks.

This brilliant plan of mine started with me waiting for my mom to leave for work. I'd go across the street to my neighbor's apartment, Ms. Lamar,[8] where I babysat. I would go back to sleep, wake up for breakfast, watch soap operas, and return home as if I had been at school all day.

I met Ms. Lamar through Grandma Ruby, who had referred me to her for babysitting. We became good friends, so I felt comfortable executing my plan at her apartment. But fun times must come to an end as reality rears its head.

Well, see, what happened was that life of luxury abruptly stopped. We did not have a landline, and cell phones did not exist so the school would send truancy letters to my house. Little Miss Postmaster here would get the mail, read the letter, and then trash it. The things we do when we want our way!

I thought I had gotten away with skipping school until I returned and was summoned to the attendance office. Due to phone issues, they couldn't reach my mother, and they were worried because they hadn't received a response to their letters.

"Tammy, we've been sending letters to your home and still have not heard from your mother. Please give her this note regarding your extreme absences. If your mother does not respond promptly, we will send truancy officers to your home. Do you understand?" Mrs. Dunphy asked.[9]

"Do I understand? Do I understand? Yeah, I understood that once I gave Momma this note, I would meet Jesus!" In retrospect, I felt like John Coffey in the Green Mile, and I could see the electric chair with my name hanging over it. This was not good.

Life with Mom

Well, I was in it now; there was no turning back. I knew I had to hand over this proof of my poor judgment about school.

I handed Momma the letter and waited for life as I knew it to end. Fortunately for me, she had received salvation and was in the process of changing her old ways, and she spared me the beating I deserved. However, we did have to visit City Hall and speak with the truancy officers. Momma had my two sisters and their babies to contend with; a reckless daughter was a bit too much.

"Tammy, it pains to do this, but Grandma says that I have to send you back to her because it was never your desire to come here in the first place."

Okay, Tammy, don't act so happy," I told myself. However, out loud, I said, "I'm sorry, Momma, but I understand what you have to do."

I know God works miracles, but I had always been curious as to why Momma didn't peel my skin from my backside. We talked about this some years ago.

"Momma, I often think about my little plan of skipping school and wonder why you didn't punish me."

"Oh, baby girl, I could see the fear in your eyes. God told me not to punish you and that He'd take care of it."

Momma was obedient, but my genius plan meant I still had to pay for the consequences of missing school by repeating the eighth grade.

Chapter 3

There's No Place Like Home

I felt like Dorothy from The Wizard of Oz when she clicked her heels three times and woke up in her bed back in Kansas. Everyone she knew and loved was there for her.

Well, after a bit of my own drama, I made it back to Niagara Falls, where I, too, felt overwhelmed with delight to return to familiar surroundings. This is where I was comfortable, and this is when I started regularly attending church.

I had not yet joined the choir, but I had been permitted to travel with them in Chicago and Detroit. I was ecstatic. Our first destination was Pastor Baker's church in Chicago. The service was incredibly uplifting, and the presence of the Lord was intense. It felt like a spiritual revival, and the message deeply touched me. That day, I strongly felt it was the right time. So, when the altar call was made with the invitation to Christ, I didn't hesitate to go to the altar and accept Jesus Christ as my Lord and Savior.

Now, it was time to reset my young life. I had to repeat the 8th grade; it was no one's fault but my own. But I was determined to live for Christ, which meant taking care of my education.

I rejoined my friends and began developing into the person I was meant to be. I still didn't know what God had called me for, but I knew it would change lives, and I was content with that for the moment.

My life with Christ had given me confidence like never before, and I became more adventurous in going outdoors. One day, I met two of our neighbors, Michael and Mark, who were around my age. We became friends, and they looked out for me like I was their sister.

I fell into a new routine that looked like this: school during the week, Sunday morning worship and Sunday night service, Monday night Bible study, Tuesday choir rehearsal, Wednesday night service, and Friday night service, and then all over again on Sunday.

I stayed busy working in different church auxiliaries but kept a low profile at school. I joined the church choir, served on the usher board, and eventually worked with the Tape Ministry and the bookstore before becoming the choir director.

I wholeheartedly loved the Lord and was determined to serve Him. Life wasn't always easy, but overall, I found joy in serving God as a young person.

There's No Place Like Home

This afforded me an opportunity to meet many people at the revivals. Church was so good; it was my life at that time. I didn't know there was more out there for me because I had been sheltered for most of my life.

I found that a turnaround had taken place, as I was no longer merely existing, but I had embarked on a journey of spiritual growth in Christ that has shaped me into the person I am today. Now that I'm older, I can see the hand of God in my life. I grew stronger in God through Bible study and spending time in His Word. As I grew spiritually stronger, I noticed things in my life began to change, and I was finally in a place where I accepted myself and felt I belonged.

It's beautiful how the love of God can heal us without actually seeing it happen. All I know is that I didn't feel like an outsider anymore. Gone was the shame about my height and hair; people accepted me because I accepted myself. I had disembarked from that cave and been made free in my mind, body, and soul. When people saw me, they saw the love of God and its transformative work making its way to purpose.

Financially, my grandparents struggled and did their best. But people notice when you don't wear nice church clothes. What I mean by that is this: Back then, I was a member of a Pentecostal church with strict dress codes. Women and girls wore skirts or dresses only, no pants.

There was no coming as you are with whatever clothes you owned. No, there was a strict expectation about their concept of being "holy." I have since learned the truth about "church attire." But even through that, God used people to bless me with proper clothing.

As time progressed, if there was such a thing, the downside was that I lost many friends, which hurt. I didn't know then that God was pruning my life of those who weren't going in the same direction. Believers often fail to see that when God closes a door, He opens another one, a better one. Therefore, when people walk away from you, purging is needed for that season of your life. However, He always brings other people into your life for His reasons, seasons, and some for a lifetime. No matter how long they're in your life, it's for God's purpose, but sometimes the cost is pain.

If you recall, I spent a lot of time alone in my preteen years. But like He does, God blessed me to find new friends who were about to travel my same path of salvation. This new set of God-sent friends enjoyed similar interests as me, like hanging out and singing after church, attending midnight musicals, participating in community choirs with other young people, and traveling. This new life in Christ was a whole new world, and I was happy to be in it.

Getting My Education

By the time I reached high school, I was a loner. I wore dresses that were not popular then, and I always carried my Bible. Principal Jones[10] took notice and allowed me to assist with office work, and that's how I would spend my lunch hour each day.

By graduation, I was working and making my own money. It felt good to finally buy new clothes and help my grandparents, who had done a great job with me.

Graduation was scheduled for 1985, and I wanted to attend college in Atlanta, Georgia, so I applied to Clark University and was accepted. However, Grandma Ruby and Momma disagreed with my plan. Their concern was that we didn't have family there, and they didn't want me to be alone. Alone? That's been going on for most of my life. I think I would have been...Wait. I KNOW I would have been just fine. Just the same, I was hometown-bound. It wasn't long before I became comfortable doing the same thing every day, along with many of my friends at church. Now I can see that, again, I didn't use my voice and gave in to their decision for me to remain in Niagara Falls.

The Church Life

As a young girl, God's love for me mattered because I felt unloved by my family. So, when He called me into His purpose by saying, "It's time," those were the most beautiful words I could hear. I began to hear those words frequently and with more power. However, I still didn't understand what was meant by what He said.

How did "It's Time" connect to my purpose? I didn't have anyone to help me understand what was going on. In retrospect, I thought about Samuel when he was a little boy, and when he first heard from the Lord, he kept running to Eli because he didn't understand what was happening. Eli explained to him that the Lord was calling him. Of course, Samuel was in the temple, so his call made sense. But here I was, estranged from my mom and my sisters, living with my grandparents with no clue as to what was happening in my life.

For several years, our church community was bustling with young people, and we made the most of it by organizing delightful bus trips and road excursions with the choir. Following our church gatherings on Friday evenings, we would assemble at different homes, relishing each other's company. I eagerly looked forward to our shut-ins, which meant women only, which was the practice of my church.

Our interactions were never about pursuing romantic relationships; our deep love united us for God and genuine enjoyment of one another's presence.

Our church's foundation was God-based; our pastor really believed in that. We were blessed to have quite a few older women pour their experience, knowledge, and wisdom into us young people. The Bible tells us they are to teach the young, and they did. They truly followed Titus 2:3-5, **The aged women likewise, that they be in behaviour as becometh holiness, not false accusers, not given to much wine, teachers of good things; ⁴That they may teach the young women to be sober, to love their husbands, to love their children, ⁵To be discreet, chaste, keepers at home, good, obedient to their own husbands, that the word of God be not blasphemed.**

Of course, some of the younger people laughed about the teachings, but I took them seriously and began spending more time with the older, Spirit-filled people. I was in hot pursuit of God and was trying to pick up a little wisdom here and there. I was determined not to lose any footing and to stay with Him.

I love God with all my heart, and I couldn't see myself doing anything else but serving Him. I could not see my life without God then, and I certainly cannot see my life without Him now. Salvation at 13 was good, but I wish I had been saved long before then because of the drastic change within me. But then again, I sometimes forget it is all about God's timing. We are on His divine time, and not ours.

The Servant's Heart

By the time I was sixteen or seventeen, I noticed that my friends had started drifting from regular attendance and backsliding to a life filled with partying. In a very short time, I lost the friendship of my three best friends because we were no longer headed in the same direction.

Also, during this time, it didn't matter where I sat in church; when there was a visiting prophet, I was called out for them to speak about my life. I can testify that most of what was said in prophecy has come to pass.

So, I began working with the youth choirs and helping out with the babies and toddlers of the women who were mentoring me. My lap was never empty for holding somebody's baby or helping out with the children, which was awesome to watch the young people grow up.

Teenagers also came to me to talk about their lives. And there I was, operating in a season of purpose without realizing it.

Here I was about four years later; the tall, awkward, and unattractive girl who had been bullied now had followers, young girls at the church who would actually mimic my praise and hold their hands like me. I felt seen, and people noticed my love for the Lord.

Because I hung around the choir, I eventually became the youth choir director and ended up in the adult choir as a strong alto. Yes, that's right. The same little girl who thought she had no voice was blasting out the praises of God in song.

And yet another change that took place in our congregation was that many young people were getting married, having babies, and moving on with their lives. It seemed like everyone was getting married except for me. I never wanted to date anyone at my church because I always saw those guys as brothers, not potential spouses. Therefore, I began my journey of purity and faithfulness to God by attending church and enjoying life as a single woman; however, deep down inside, I knew I wanted more.

Once again, I had another brilliant plan. Like I said, I wanted marriage, but not to anyone local. I preferred a long-distance relationship. My reason was that since I was a virgin, I wanted to remain that way until marriage. I wanted to give this precious gift to my husband.

I anticipated that dating someone from my church or in my local area would pose challenges due to the temptation involved. I was committed to staying celibate until marriage. Therefore, I decided to pursue long-distance relationships to avoid succumbing to temptation. My strategy initially seemed effective, but it ultimately led to unexpected consequences.

Signs & Wonders

At this time, I wasn't thinking about relationships, and women were hating on me at church and telling their husbands not to talk to me. They were so far from the truth; as I stated, I wanted a long-distance relationship.

Things turned so bad that one woman tried to trip me as I passed by her in the pew, while another one actually spat in my hair. It seemed the more I pursued the Lord, the worse I was treated by the women who claimed to love Him.

I later learned many cherished and highly respected me and referred to me as "The Bethlehem Princess," which was a huge compliment. The few outnumbered the many who saw the genuineness of my heart for the people.

As I sit and think about the Word of God and His awesomeness, I'm reminded of a day when I was walking home after Bible study with two of the brothers from my church. I must have been around my early 20s.

Carl and John walked me home that night and stopped in the parking lot outside my apartment. Naturally, we had been talking about the Lord on the walk, and the conversation was so good that we continued lifting the name of the Lord in the parking lot.

The next day, my sister Janice, who lived in the apartments across the street from me, asked, "Tammy, who were those men you talked to last night?"

"It was Carl and John from the church."

"Well, who was the fourth person with y'all?" she asked.

"Girl, get your eyes checked. It was only the three of us," I responded.

Adamant about what she saw, Janice continued, "Naw, Tammy, I saw four people. I even yelled to Ryan to ask him who the other person was. When Ryan entered the room and looked out of the window, he said, 'I see Tammy, John, and Carl, but I don't know who that other person is.'"

I said that to say this: Matthew 18:20, Jesus said, *"For where two or three are gathered together in my name, there am I in the midst of them."*

Excuse me while I give Him some praise. Hallelujah! I praise You, Lord God Almighty!

Though we hear the Scriptures, we don't always make them personal. But hear me when I tell you that we should!

Take a moment and think of the many times you and your friends got together and just lifted the name of Jesus, not fully realizing He was in the midst. We read and hear the Scriptures in church, but what percentage of what we read do we actually believe?

Chapter 4

WHO DID I MARRY?

The words of his mouth were smoother than cream or butter, but war was in his heart; his words were softer than oil, yet they were drawn swords (Psalms 55:21, AMPC).

In 1992, at the age of 26, I found myself fully immersed in the activities of the church and its choir. Our busy schedule led us to a convention in New York City, where we took the opportunity to visit a church in the Bronx. The visit left a lasting impression on me with its warmth and beauty. During this convention, I was introduced to a man named Gerard by a fellow church member. To my surprise, he boldly claimed, "I'm going to marry that girl. I'm going to marry Tammy." Initially, I was put off by his arrogance, as it was common for guys to make playful jabs to evoke a reaction. Despite my reluctance, I consistently matched his banter with my own retorts.

I don't know what happened. I don't know if I felt bad about ever getting married because all my friends were. Whatever it was, I was beginning to feel some pressure.

A short time later, I attended a friend's wedding in South Carolina. Who else would be there other than Gerard?

Was this a coincidence or a set-up? I had no idea. But there he was, with his overly confident self as usual.

I engaged in a polite conversation and must credit him for his persistence. We began talking, and I started to feel comfortable with him. Like many young women, I entertained the idea of a life with him. Things progressed, and before long, we started a long-distance relationship. He would visit me wherever I traveled, and I would sometimes visit him in New York.

After about a year, he proposed, followed by a year-long engagement, and we were married. At first, I was so excited about getting married, moving away to a big city, and being a submissive wife—you know, all the bells and whistles that a young girl dreams of, which eventually turned out to be a nightmare.

Houston, We Have a Problem!

For it is not an enemy who reproaches and taunts me—then I might bear it; nor is it one who has hated me who insolently vaunts himself against me—then I might hide from him. [13] But it was you, a man my equal, my companion and my familiar friend. [14] We had sweet fellowship together and used to walk to the house of God in company (Psalms 55:12-14, AMPC).

In the year 1996, at the age of 29, I tied the knot with Gerard and embarked on a new chapter in my life by relocating to Atlanta with him. The prospect of this move filled me with a mix of excitement and apprehension, knowing that I was venturing away from the familiar comforts of home, my family, and my church community. It was a time of great change and uncertainty, but also one filled with hope and anticipation for the future.

Like most marriages, ours was good at first. But then "life" happened. We had one car to share between the two of us. Gerard worked all the time, and initially, I was home because of the conflict of me having a career.

When Gerard and I first met, I was an independent, adventurous woman with a career. I was taken aback when I learned he wanted me to be a stay-at-home wife. Thankfully, my employer offered me the opportunity to relocate to an Atlanta store, but Gerard was not open to this idea. Our discussions often revolved around his insistence that I remain at home.

"Gerard, I've got to work. I'm used to having my own money."

"Well, you've got a husband to take care of that now."

"But the company found a position for me here, and I put in for the transfer. They are expecting me to show up for work…"

His response, "I don't care about that, you don't need to be working at a men's store."

As I ponder quietly, the scene evokes memories of a 1940s movie in which the woman stays home to cook and clean while the man goes off to work.

How did we stray so far from the Word of God, twisting and distorting it to fit our narrow perspectives? For example, in the Pentecostal community, many interpret God's assignment of work to Adam before Eve as a mandate for men to exclusively provide for their families. However, this overlooks the powerful message in Proverbs 31, which praises a woman who manages her household and engages in business and community work. In Acts 8:26-39, a Queen of Candace in Ethiopia was mentioned. In the book of Judges, we can also read about Deborah, who stood in the office of judge, warrior, and wife. Please don't misunderstand; this is not a critique of Pentecostal beliefs, as I wouldn't be who I am today without some of its teachings. However, this serves to demonstrate that God never intended to restrict women from pursuing careers and how easily we confuse man's doctrine from Scripture taken out of context.

Now, don't get me wrong. If a Sistah wants to stay home, hey, girl, do your thing! I applaud you. But as for me, well, you get the drift.

So, there we were; neither of us had this knowledge, so chaos about my work ensued. "You need to quit because you are a woman, and you have no business working in a men's department store. It doesn't look right."

Therefore, Mrs. Naïve, who grew up hearing how a wife is supposed to be submissive to her husband, did it. Little did I know that submissiveness had nothing to do with the dictatorship I was under. What I failed to do is what most women fail to do, which was my research on submission at the time. What did God have to say about submission in His Word? I didn't ask Him and followed what "man" had put in place instead and became miserable.

Gerard beating the proverbial "dead horse" about the job made my first year away from Niagara Falls quite tricky. It would be a challenge to start building my own life here. I would have to figure it out.

There I was, a small-town girl, newly married, needing to learn the life of the big city of Atlanta. My husband was tripping, and I had no friends here; I felt like a fish out of water. I couldn't catch my breath. On top of that, I was alone at home all day. I had no car to venture out in or money to spend if I found somewhere to go.

Oh, I was still connected to my family because I called them every day (smiling). They were my lifeline. I remember Gerard fussing about the phone bill because it was so high. (LOL) Yes, it was! However, I cried and became more miserable until this small-town woman realized I could use phone cards purchased from the local gas station. This movement of freedom gave me the space I needed to call Grandma Ruby, Momma, Janice, Lisa, and my friends. I even reached out to my pastor.

I stayed home for about a year and climbed the walls from boredom. Gerard was at work all day, and I was stuck at home with no money or transportation. I wanted my own money and independence, so I kept asking him about getting a job, and the answer was always "No."

My husband wanted me to stay home, but I wanted to work. This was new to me, as I had been doing housework all day, and there's only so much you can do. And then there was drama when Gerard came home and ignored me because he said he was tired. When he came home, he only wanted to eat dinner and relax.

I couldn't see the fairness in it. Since he had worked all day, I had been cleaning and cooking dinner in the house, so I wanted to go out.

I was somewhat handicapped because I was not yet familiar with the area. He used this to his advantage, cultivating a lonely life for me in the house.

I ran out of phone cards and started making calls again, running up the phone bill because I needed to hear my loved ones' voices.

I was doing my best to be a good wife, operating in submission as I understood it. I wasn't trying to be difficult, but in my opinion, having two incomes in a household is always better than having just one. I knew this from the years I spent with my grandparents.

I was beginning to feel like I was under house arrest, and all I was missing was the ankle monitor. Therefore, asking to go out was met with a "We can't afford it, or we don't have the money to do this, or we don't have the money to do that." And I found myself giving in to this, which was draining my soul.

Afterward, I was firm in my stance on the matter, and the more I discussed it with Gerard and tried to convey my feelings, the less he seemed to listen. Once again, I felt invisible, and another bookmark was stamped on my brain and in my heart. Sometimes, I required money to purchase personal items or go to a nearby store. When I brought this up, he would barrage me with questions. "What do you need from the store that I can't pick up for you? How much is it going to cost? And how long will you be gone?"

It was becoming painfully apparent that he needed control. However, I got tired of him pushing me into this emotional corner. I came out fighting, saying, "I need to work!"

Thank God for Jesus! My next-door neighbor, Sandra,[11] befriended me, and I started getting out of the house and riding around town with her, and you know Gerard didn't like that. He said that she was an unsaved single woman, and I had no business being around her.

He preferred that I remain in the house all day, and again, I didn't realize that I was being controlled. But I didn't know any better. No one ever taught me anything about control. This was the first relationship I had ever been in, and so I didn't know anything about men who had been taught that he was supposed to keep his wife in check. This was nothing but manipulation. I had never seen this before, so I didn't know what it looked like. I've since made a promise to myself to help others in this area. We must be about our Father's business by preparing our sons and daughters for relationships, and this doesn't start in their teen years. No, we must be on the bandwagon of love when they are babies as we give them unconditional love and direction. We must train them up!

What a Girl Wants

You would think that I would have been prepared for the next chapter in this man's game, but I wasn't. My hanging out with Sandra brought on more negative conversations about what I could or could not do.

"Tammy, I don't know this Sandra chick, and I don't want you traipsing around the city with her," he said gruffly.

"Gerard, I don't know anyone here and need to make friends. I can't do that by sitting in the house all day. I'm thankful to God that He sent me Sandra," I said sadly.

Then one thing led to another, and the list started to grow with his, "You can't go there, and you can't wear that." He had an issue with me wearing pants, of all things. What is it with these religious rules? We've got to do better about understanding the Word of God.

Anyway, I had had enough and took matters into my own hands by filling out employment applications. Right off the bat, the bank hired me. Sadly, I had to carpool with different people to get to training classes and then take the bus from the bank back home, but it was worth the effort. The weight of no personal transportation and no job had been heavy. I refused to live like that any longer.

I have a job! I was excited about having my own money again. I enjoyed the work, and it was nice getting out, meeting new people, and regaining some control over my life again. This new attitude gave me the confidence to apply for another job at an airline because that's where I've always wanted to work.

So, I knew I had pushed the envelope by moving ahead and accepting the job from the bank. Trying to be respectful, I approached Gerard with my plan.

"Babe, I was offered a position at an airline today."

Grunting like he was constipated, "Really? Doing what exactly?"

"A flight attendant," I rushed my response.

"Oh, Naw, Tam, that ain't going to work. You can't be a flight attendant."

He didn't say I couldn't work for the airlines; he just said I couldn't be a flight attendant. Therefore, I applied for a ground job at the airline, and I prayed and prayed and prayed for this job. I even called my father, Pastor Walter Grooms,[12] and had him pray and fast with me because I wanted it.

Let me pause and tell you a little about this man the Lord sent into my life.

Who Did I Marry?

Momma and Dad met in middle school when they were young. Momma said that as they grew up, he had taken on some habits that had turned her off, so she wanted no part of him.

So, after all these years, Aunt Lynn invited Momma to church. By this time, Dad was known as Pastor Walter Grooms. When Momma got to church and saw him in the pulpit, she leaned over to Aunt Lynn and said, "Why is that drunk doing in the pulpit?"

Aunt Lynn laughed and said, "He's a changed man now."

Long story short, Mom was surprised to see how Dad had changed, and she was later saved.

In the meantime, the Lord was dealing with Dad and told him that Momma was his wife and that she was to be his helpmate with the church he was to start.

Honestly, I didn't like him at first. Mom and I had missed many years together, and now that we were reunited, I wasn't ready to let her go. Another one of my brilliant plans was executed at their wedding. I was so indignant that when he lifted her veil, I kissed her on the cheek before he could. LOL! Lord, thank you for a changed heart.

From Pain to Purpose

But let me tell you that Dad has more than proven himself. In my book, he is the best Dad ever!

He said, "Tammy, I don't know who your real father was, but he missed out on a jewel."

He was there when I had Carrie and throughout my pregnancy. To me, Dad is the best man on this earth that has happened to me. He showed me what a loving father was supposed to be. He was a father, best friend, counselor, and pastor.

Again, excuse my passion. I had to share this to let you know that God is a provider and will give you the desires of your heart when you live a life of holiness.

Now, back to the job situation. Life lesson number 2,190,001. To show you how God operates, we think He will come one way and then we find that He shows up in another. So after I applied for the job, we prayed and fasted, and I got a rejection letter letting me know there was no offer for employment. I did not get an interview, so there was no job. I was crushed, and I didn't understand how, with all the praying and fasting, there was yet another "No" in my life. Talk about spiritual immaturity.

I called my father then, and we discussed the outcome. He could not give me a definitive answer on why God didn't answer my prayer. However, a few months later, Dad had to go to South Dakota for a pastor's conference. He didn't feel up to going, but he still attended. He met and introduced himself to the pastor seated next to him. They became engrossed in conversation, and he found out the pastor was from Atlanta and happened to work for Airlines!

Dad told him my story, and the pastor told him to have me reapply for the job, but this time, I was to use the pastor's name as a reference. I did, and I got a call for an interview. I said that to say this: God will always get the glory out of our situations, and this is just one of the many in my life. He sent my father to South Dakota, to the proper connection, so that I could be hired at Delta. I praise Him because I've been with the company for 28 years.

If you're praying for something, continue to pray. Our pastor always said, "**P.U.S.H.**" - **P**ray **U**ntil **S**omething **H**appens. God is not a God that he should lie (Numbers 23:19). His word will not return unto Him void. It will complete its mission (Isaiah 55:12). Hang in there, continue to trust God with all your heart, and don't lean on your own understanding (Proverbs 3:5-6). God's ways are not our ways, and we will never understand His mind because we're not like Him (Isaiah 55:8-9).

What's Yours is Mine

My work life had improved as I started working for Delta in 1997 and began meeting people and making friends. It was exciting because I was finally coming into my own and learning big city life. Was I scared? Absolutely. I was nervous, but God connected me with some great people, some great co-workers, and a lot of seasoned agents who were there to guide me and teach me the ropes, and I am forever thankful to every one of them.

My home life—well, we were still using one car, so I had to carpool with a phenomenal friend, Cheryl. She never complained, sweet as she could be, but sometimes, our schedules conflicted. There were times I had to wait for her shift to end, and there were times she had to wait for me. But if Cheryl or others I carpooled with had something else to do, I wondered how I would get home.

Riding home one day, out of the blue, Cheryl asked, "Tammy, you're working now, so why not buy a car?

I know Cheryl's heart, and she wanted the best for me. This was by no means an effort to kick me out of her car. No, she could see how much I needed my independence, so she was reluctant to drop the subject of my getting a car. However, one day, the message would come through loud and clear. And so, she would ask, "Tammy, why don't you get yourself a car?"

"I talked to my husband about it, and he said no, that I didn't need a car right now."

She became quiet and moved away from that subject for a while. About a year later, she returned to me and said, "Tammy, why don't you get yourself a car?"

Again, I replied, "Gerard is against me having my own car."

I had been working for a year; by now, I should have bought a vowel and figured it out. I had the income, and it was time to buy a car!

Finally, Cheryl had had enough. She asked once more, and I answered, "Look, Sis, I appreciate your desire for me, but Gerard is against me getting a car."

Without missing a beat, she looked at me and said, "Forget him! We're going to get you a car."

We left work and headed to a car lot. A little paperwork, my signature, and I drove away with my first brand-new car. Now, if you're familiar with Atlanta traffic, then you know it can be scary, but I was so happy to have my own car and the freedom to come and go, and I was pleased that I drove home a new woman.

When Gerard arrived home that evening, I was excited about my news.

"I bought a car today," I was so excited I was almost out of breath.

He didn't skip a beat, "Don't ask me to do anything to help you with this car; you're on your own!"

Who did I marry? What was this man's problem? Instead of applauding my independence, he decided to step on it. His comment hurt because I didn't understand why he didn't want me to have a car. I still didn't get that he was trying to limit my freedom so he could continue controlling me. After all, this was not his first attempt at control. Before our wedding, we agreed to purchase our condo together, but I was edged out of that when he put his mother's name in place of mine, and I spent the next few years asking to have my name added. It never happened!

This happens when we get married without talking to people who have been married a long time and have experienced some real-life issues. Traditional marriage counseling needs to change to hard-hitting questions about one's spiritual, mental, and emotional state. Hindsight is 20-20, but I'm equipped to help others now.

So, he put his foot down about my car. Well, I won't talk about how his car broke down. Okay, I changed my mind (LOL).

Who Did I Marry?

I was at a friend's birthday dinner when I arrived home. Gerard was very irritated and troubled because… guess what? His car had broken down, and he had to walk home. You know they say that God doesn't like ugly (behavior)…

Well, the freedom of the new car was short-lived. Because he negatively opened his mouth, his car broke down, so I would have to get him to work. Once again, we were on the one-car repeat cycle.

Needless to say, I was in my feelings because I didn't want to return to that cycle. What was going on?

I would get up early in the morning, drop him off at his job, and then drive to mine. After a long day, I would come home to fix dinner, and then I had to leave and pick him up from his job. It was tough for a while, all that back and forth. My emotions were everywhere, and I often wanted to say, "Get to work the best way you can." But I remembered the Word in Romans 12:18, *"If it be possible as much as lieth in you, live peaceably with all men."* So, I sucked it up, and I took him to work.

I guess it wasn't enough that I found a job and bought a car; he had to find something to control. Therefore, he once more dredged up that old religious doctrine of "no wearing pants." Again, we take God's Word out of context. Let's take a look at it. *"A woman is not to wear male clothing, and a man is not to put on a woman's garment, for everyone who does these things is detestable to the Lord your God* (Deuteronomy 22:5 CEB).

God said a woman should not wear clothes made for a man, and vice-versa. Well, let's look at this for a moment. Back in the biblical times, everyone wore robes. How did they determine which robes were for men and which were for women? Just like in today's fashion, their robes are tailored according to gender. The women had long flowing robes, brighter colors, more feminine. Meanwhile, the men's robes were dull colors and plain fabric. So, when God said that a woman wasn't supposed to wear men's clothing, it wasn't pants because they had not yet been invented. It was about not wearing the clothes of the opposite sex to hide your true gender. We see this every day.

Y'all, excuse me, I'm full right now. God has opened my eyes and liberated me with the truth!

My church back home honored this thought process, but I wanted to wear pants anyway. And I did.

Our airline uniforms looked nice with a dress, skirt, or pants, so I devised a plan once again. I would put my pants in the locker to change into the skirt before I went home. Looking back, I see how naïve I was. I'd say I was trying to keep the peace, but was I really? In hindsight, I feel like a kid sneaking and doing something against my parents' will. But this is what happens when we don't have a good understanding of God's Word, and we fall into the traditions of man. We end up in relationships that can cripple our hearts, minds, and souls.

And That's Mine Too!

Mr. Gerard decided he was not torturing me enough, so he took his game to another level. I was working, had my new car, doing my thing with my pants, and then he dropped the hammer.

"Tammy, I need you to give me your paycheck from now on."

I was stunned.

"What?"

"You heard me; I will pay all the bills."

Now, he thinks I am Boo-Boo the Fool's sister. I can count. He was paying bills before I got a job. Why the torture, Lord?

I gave in....

Once again, I found myself facing an extension to my time in confinement. Despite being a fully independent woman with a successful career, I still lacked the freedom to

From Pain to Purpose

access my finances without asking Mr. ATM. I must admit, the situation was daunting. I felt apprehensive about speaking up due to his consistent tendency to react with anger and unleash hurtful, verbally abusive remarks. Whoever coined the phrase "Sticks and stones may break my bones, but words will never hurt me" couldn't have been more mistaken. The actual words to that rhyme are:

"Sticks and stones may break my bones, but words can also hurt me. Stones and sticks break only skin, while words are ghosts that haunt me. Slant and curved the word-swords fall, it pierces and sticks inside me. Bats and bricks may ache through bones, but words can mortify me. Pain from words has left its' scar, on mind and hear that's tender. Cuts and bruises have not healed, it's words that I remember."[13]

As you can see from this childhood poem, someone felt the pain of words and penned them. Words hurt and have lasting scars when we don't know who we are in Christ. Again, it is imperative to read the Word for yourself. It's great that we have spiritual leaders, but you must incorporate the Word at some point in your walk.

Looking back on my life, it is reminiscent of the scenes from "The Color Purple," when Mister always slung degrading words at Celie, leaving her wounded.

As women, we take this kind of treatment, and we take it, and we take it. Listen, it was not easy to hear my husband say negative things to me. He didn't listen when I talked, making me feel I should be seen and not heard unless guests were in our home. Of course, this is when he would put on his show, putting on his best behavior.

I thank God for his mother, Ms. Gladys.[14] She was always good to me. If there was anything I needed or wanted, all I had to do was talk with her. She would call him, and after speaking to her, things would change - for a moment. But by now, I was wising up, and I knew this act wasn't real.

Ms. Gladys told me to stop giving him my check and give him what I wanted him to have toward the bills. I had worked for it, and the rest belonged to me. Much to his surprise, I stopped. I cut him off. Was he happy? Not by a long shot. We had a massive disagreement about that. But I had to do what I needed to do for myself, and I did so bit by bit.

Other marital issues included isolation, but he was good at that. We spent very little time together as a couple. We went on maybe two trips, but anytime I asked about getting away and going somewhere and trying to create a romantic setting so we could get refreshed, he always had a reason not to.

It made no sense that we weren't going anywhere. I was not used to this; something had to change. I worked for an airline; why would I not travel?

I would mentally escape while at work, looking up different resources, places, and things about planning a getaway for the two of us, ensuring it was within our budget. I would go back to him with the plan, and Gerard always said his usual, "No, Tammy, we can't afford that trip. We can't do this. We don't have the money for that."

I now see that it was a form of punishment for not following his every command. However, I didn't give up on us; I continued to work on the marriage.

Subsequently, I reached the point where I stopped arguing with him, feeling that things would be better, and we would be okay. Let him say whatever he wanted to say; I'd deal with it; don't respond, and maybe the relationship would improve. I was wrong on all accounts.

Chapter 5

LIFE BE LIFING - (PT. 1)

Well, I tried to keep quiet for a few months. It was going okay—not well, but okay. I'm shocked to make the connection, because this is what I did as a child when I felt I had no voice. I balled myself up and tucked myself away to keep what I thought was peace in my home. Then, my proverbial light came on, and I had this brilliant idea that things would improve if I had a baby.

I don't know why we women think that having a baby will fix a broken relationship. In addition to that thought, it was hard for me to get pregnant at first. We were married for about three years before I got pregnant. I never took any birth control, and we didn't use any protection. I found out I had fibroid tumors, and surgery was needed to prevent the fibroid tumor from growing along with the fetus, which could cause premature labor or miscarriage. I wanted a baby. Therefore, I proceeded with the surgery, and one year later, I got pregnant.

This was a genuinely rocky time in my marriage. The dictator and his rules were toxic, to say the least. But I didn't let that rain on my parade. I was excited to become a mom.

There was something special about knowing life was growing inside me. I was so blessed.

Morning sickness was horrible, but once I got over it, I resumed my happiness about my pregnancy. There are no words to describe that feeling. It's a miracle, and I will be forever grateful to God for Carrie.

Just writing about this brings tears to my eyes because it was one of the happiest times of my life, even while living in a tyrannical environment. I can remember lying in bed, with her moving around in my belly, and me reading the book of Proverbs to her. Laying there and caring for my unborn child, I thought about the good things I wanted for her in life. I was not in a position to say what I wanted her to be; only God could do that. But I would adhere to raising her in His way, impart knowledge, and share wisdom with my baby.

My Girl!

The C-section was scheduled for September 24, 2000; however, on September 7th, I was home alone, watching TV. I remember watching a movie with Bruce Willis, and I thought I had a little cramp in my stomach. I didn't pay any attention at first, and because it was my first pregnancy, I remembered being told that labor pains can feel like cramps.

Life Be Lifing (Pt. 1)

I waited a few minutes, and the cramp started again. Gerard was working, so I thought I'd track how far apart they were coming. At first, it was every 20 minutes. Then, it was every 15 minutes, and I knew it was time to call my doctor. I wanted to ensure everything was okay because I knew the baby wasn't due for a few more weeks.

Dr. Lansing[15] instructed me to come to the hospital; I called Gerard. He came home, and we went to the hospital. When I got there, the doctor checked me and said that I had already dilated 3 centimeters, and if I got to 7 centimeters, I would have the baby vaginally.

When I had the fibroid tumor removed a year earlier, I was told then that a C-section would be necessary when it came time for delivery. Having the baby vaginally would be a high risk. Naturally, I agreed to a C-section to make sure both of us would be healthy....

Like Hannah returned Samuel to God, I said, "Lord, I give her back to you." So, by the age of two, I kept her in church, and during that time, Gerard and I were building a house.

My next-door neighbor was kind enough to look after Carrie for me while I went to check on the new house. When I returned for Carrie, Sandra seemed perplexed. I could tell something had happened.

"Tammy, I'm not sure what I witnessed today. But Carrie gathered all her dolls and stuffed animals and put them at the bottom of the stairs while she stood over them and had church."

Obviously, this moved Sandra's spirit, as she continued, "She was standing there singing hallelujah, clapping her hands, and praising God, and I didn't know what to do."

Talk about a proud Momma. My baby had been paying attention to worship service and what I had taught her at home.

It is important to instill a belief in God in your children from a young age. Carrie loved church, and even in her teenage years, it was, you know, "Mom, are we going to church?" She would ask me to drop her off if I was sick and didn't feel like going. She loves church. She loves God, and I'm grateful to Him for that.

So, Gerard and I created this beautiful daughter, and I thought things would get better in my marriage. It did not stop the arguing, and he continued to be distant and not spend time with our daughter at the park or go for a walk for the two of us. Nada! No family memories were being created. I didn't want this for her because I had already lived it.

Life Be Lifing (Pt. 1)

The few times we dined out, we looked at our plates and other people in the restaurant. There was this awkward silence, and he refused to communicate with me about anything except what he wanted. It wasn't good, and I tried to stick it out. I suggested counseling, but he responded, "I'm not talking to a counselor. They don't pay my bills."

In 2003, we moved into our new house, and Carrie was three then. I knew my daughter was special, but I saw something extra when Gerard and I argued one day. All of a sudden, she started singing and praising God. This became her practice each time he and I were at odds. She would break out in praise and would sing worship songs.

It did something to my heart. I pointed this out to Gerard and said, listen to your daughter, and it was then I realized that I could not continue in this madness. I did not want my daughter to grow up in a home with no love and no displays of affection. Sadly, Carrie had never seen me and her dad hug, and that's not what I envisioned life for my child.

My desire was for my child(ren) to grow up with both parents in the home, but that wouldn't happen. I finally summoned the courage to make up my mind that I was going to leave. I hadn't said anything to anyone. I hadn't shared it with anybody, but it was a decision I made for myself. Enough was enough. It was time to put a plan in place.

Intruder Alert!

Installing a security system in your home is good, especially when the alarm sounds, "Intruder Alert!" This is to warn you that someone is trying to break into your home. Upon hearing the warning, your adrenaline increases in preparation for a fight or flight. Likewise, we must be discerning about those men and women who wish to intrude in your marriage and your personal space. Our job as married folks is not to let that happen. The man agreed to leave his parents and cleave to his wife, putting only God before her. But that was not what was happening in our home. We had an intruder, and I didn't care for him.

Gerard's so-called guy brother, Jake[16], often came into town; too much for my comfort. He was intrusive. The thing is that anytime Jake asked Gerard to do something, he'd jump up and do it. But when it came to me and what I asked for, we couldn't even go out to eat because he was always tired and didn't have the money. And there it was, another negative bookmark etched into my heart. Jake's frequent visits and Gerard's immediate compliance with his requests created a sense of imbalance in our relationship, leading to further strain.

Life Be Lifing (Pt. 1)

Now, you know, I'm thinking a lot because I've bought some vowels and have a few clues. "Why does he run and jump each time this man shows up?" But when I ask for anything, there's always a long list of why he can't do it or go anywhere with me. I had some questions as I kept my eyes on them both.

When Jake decided to move to Atlanta and wanted to stay with us, I put my foot down. I said absolutely not! So, he went to an extended-stay hotel. Okay, that's fine. But it became an issue for me when, all of a sudden, Jake locked his keys in the hotel room, but as we know, when you don't pay your bill, you can't have access, so his truck became his bedroom. And when I inquired about this mishap. They had no answer. Hmmm. I wonder why. It was always something: a place to stay, money, or some favor. Every time we turned around, his hand was out.

I'm not the jealous type, but a woman has to wonder what's going on with her man who refuses to help her but moves quickly for his friend. I finally got fed up. I asked the hard question, "What is happening with you and Jake?" Naturally, his response was filled with ranting and ravings. I never got an answer, but the situation was stressing me out because this was happening while we were trying to get pregnant.

While I was dealing with the trespasser in my house, I discovered another intruder was lurking around inside my body in the form of cancer cells on the wall of my vagina. My gynecologist did a little procedure to take care of it. A little later, a third intruder in the form of a 5-inch tumor, which was the size of a baby's head, was discovered. My physician told me that if I got pregnant, I could expect to go into premature labor or miscarry because the fibroid would grow along with the baby. This diagnosis not only posed a threat to my health but also added to the strain in our marriage, as we were already dealing with other issues.

As I shared earlier, I decided to have the surgery, which was in 1998. A few months later, I got pregnant with my daughter, who was born in 2000.

Throughout the pregnancy, our marriage became even more difficult. On the one hand, I was excited to be having a baby, but on the other, my marriage was going downhill like a roller coaster, and I did all I could to salvage it, but nothing seemed to work.

There were times when I felt the marriage would be better if I kept quiet and gave Gerard anything he wanted. Unfortunately, that did not work either. No woman ever wants her marriage to end, but sorry to say, things do happen in unsalvageable marriages when only one is doing the work. But life has a way of balancing out, and I found the strength to keep going....

You've Got What?

I was at work in 2005 when my neighbor Louise from down the street called me and said, "Tammy, you need to get home. Something has happened."

I went to my boss, explained that I had a family emergency, and he told me to leave. When I arrived home, the ambulance and paramedics were there. I questioned them about the situation, and it seemed that Gerard had a Grand-mal seizure. At that moment, I was grateful for the unexpected support from my boss and the paramedics.

He and Carrie were home, and she was playing with her toys in her room. He was in the room across the hall in the bed. According to my daughter, the bed was shaking, making a funny sound even though it shook all the time; it was an older bed. But Carrie knew that something was going on, and so she left out of her room and went in there. The scene was terrifying because a Grand-mal seizure causes you first to lose consciousness for a few seconds, followed by muscle convulsions that usually last for less than two minutes. Carrie saw this and ran out of the house to my neighbor.

Louise had several sons who had baseball or football practice every Saturday morning. However, this particular Saturday morning, Louise was running late, and as she was about to get in her car in the garage, she could hear a little girl screaming her name.

Louise ran out of her garage to see Carrie shaking and crying and instructed Carrie to go inside her house. Louise then ran to my house and found Gerard, who, during the seizure, had lost control of his bowels and was bleeding in the eyes. She called for an ambulance.

After I got the call, I made my way home. The EMTs were getting him ready for the hospital ride as I arrived, so I went to Louise's house to check on Carrie. She was shaking. She was scared. She was five. My heart shattered as she looked at me and asked, "Did daddy go be with God?"

"No, baby, he's going to the hospital."

She then proceeded to describe what she saw as best she could.

After arriving at the hospital, I called my support group. Great people I had been blessed to know. I'm glad I did because it was a long wait. About 4-5 hours later, he was stabilized and put in ICU for a couple of weeks.

The following day, I went to the hospital. I asked a doctor how he was, and the doctor said he asked him to take an HIV test, and he refused. I went into Gerard's room and said, "The doctor said you refuse to take an HIV test. Why?"

He replied, "I don't know."

"Do you think you have it?" I probed.

"I don't know," he answered.

I saw it happen. The moment my life as I knew it changed in an instant. The feeling is indescribable. I didn't know what to think or feel. My emotions were everywhere as I walked out of the hospital room. It was like I was in a fog. That was one of the worst moments of my life.

I went home and pulled Carrie close to me as I cried. I cried, and I cried; I called my parents, and they sent my sister to be by my side.

To maintain spiritual grounding and focus, Lisa placed words of encouragement around the house — on mirrors, the microwave, and the refrigerator — to remind me of God and His power.

A new cycle in my life now involved daily visits to Gerard, as I would ask, "Did you get your results?"

He'd look at me like I was speaking a foreign language and answer, "No."

From Pain to Purpose

This went on for about a week. Did he not understand the importance of this information? I didn't care who he got it from; I was concerned for Carrie's and my health.

Determined not to let this go, I called him while relaxing in the bath and asked, "Did you get your results?"

His answer was, "Yes…, and it was positive, "

I could see the nasty words of guilt as they hung in the air. I wanted to put my head under the water because there were no words for the hurt, pain, anger, and frustration I felt.

I will never forget that day as my world came crashing down. Hello, major bookmark!! I couldn't pray, I couldn't talk, I was angry, I was angry at myself, I was ashamed, I was embarrassed. And yes, most of all, I was angry with God. You heard me. I was angry with God. I don't know why we like to pretend we don't get angry with Him, but we do, and I did. The beauty of my anger is that He's a big God and made room for me to cry on His shoulder, sit in His lap, and tell Him all my troubles. He's a good, good Father. Amen.

There I was, feeling abandoned, scared, and alone, and my question was, "How did this happen? What did I do wrong that brought this misery upon me? Do I have it? Does

Life Be Lifing (Pt. 1)

my daughter have it? How can I now stay with this man knowing this?"

My first thought was to pack up and leave, but I had a five-year-old daughter who would not understand this situation. No, I could not do to her what was done to me. I did not want Carrie to grow up without her biological father like I did. How could I do that to my daughter?

Following the long list of self-inquiry was to get tested. Anxiety doesn't begin to explain what I was feeling. However, I forged ahead and praised God, and the results were negative. But there was still that nagging fear that it takes time for HIV to manifest in your body.

In 2005, when this disease hit my home, there was a worldwide HIV epidemic. On November 21, 2005, NBC News reported that more than 5 million people were affected in 2005 alone, taking the number of people *living* with HIV to 40.3 million worldwide.[17]

I tried to stay strong; I had to be strong for my daughter. She was only five; how could she possibly understand what was happening? Carrie saw the seizure; I would not add to the existing trauma she had endured.

Fight or Flight?

Needless to say, my plans to leave went right out the window. He would need care, and I would have to provide it. This was something out of a Tyler Perry movie. Do you remember in "*The Diary of a Mad Black Woman*" when Helen returned to take care of Charles after he had been shot and left paralyzed? He had dogged her out, put her out, and brought another woman into their home. Long story short, Helen took care of him, but not before she got her revenge.[18] (Chuckling), It sounds good, but I took the high road and did what was right in the sight of the Lord.

I was led to believe that I only had to care for Gerard for a month, so I took my FMLA (Family Medical Leave Act) from my job because I didn't have any family in Atlanta at the time to help with my daughter. He was on medical leave, and his checks were mailed to the house. I deposited them and paid the bills. Unfortunately, you don't get paid when you're on FMLA, so my lack of income hurt us. The mortgage, plus his illness, minus my check, wasn't looking good for us.

Gerard had been in the hospital for two weeks, and on the day I picked him up from the hospital, he accused me of stealing his money. There was no apology for his actions, jeopardizing our baby's life or mine. There was no thank you for taking care of the bills at the house or our daughter. No sir, no ma'am, no gratitude. And then the damn broke.

Transparency: I was so angry that I wanted to slap the daylight savings time out of him, but I opted for a verbal

Life Be Lifing (Pt. 1)

tsunami instead. All the rage, anger, hurt, pain, and disappointment over the years were unleashed. I let him have it up one side and down the other without ever using one curse word. Trust me, he got the message; at least, I thought he did.

His behavior in our marriage, left me questioning everything: my marriage, my existence, my purpose. "Lord, why me? What did I do in life that was so bad that I am faced with this issue?"

I was so mad that I tried to get drunk, but it didn't work. LOL! Y'all, I didn't want to feel this pain, but God told me that He wanted me to feel it all. This is that place where some would do drugs, overeat, overspend, or have promiscuous sex. How I thank God for keeping me safe even when I didn't want Him to. Those alcoholic spirits could not touch this woman of God (LOL). God told me that I could drink all I wanted, but I wouldn't get high. Well, that tantrum was short-lived!

All I could think about was removing Carrie and me from this horrible situation that Gerard had created. I wanted to leave right away, to pack up and go. My parents came for support and encouraged me to leave. They promised to help me financially and with my daughter, and I was ready to go, but I looked at this man and knew that I had to stay for a while anyway.

I had a daughter watching me, and my prayers have always been for her to grow up to be a strong woman of faith. I couldn't leave her father like that and still be the woman of God I claimed to be. I had to stay.

As for him, the damage caused by the seizures was severe; he was prohibited from driving, and so tag, I was it. Preparing his meals and ensuring he took his medicine to stop the infectious disease from taking over his body. This was the hardest thing I think I've ever had to do in my life. I questioned God with tears in my eyes every time I had to make his meals, every time I had to give him his medications, and Lord have mercy, each time I had to take him to his infectious disease (ID) doctor and sit in there with him.

I can honestly say that I hated this man at this point, but I kept trying to be an example to my daughter regardless of my feelings. I had to repeatedly remind myself that he was her father, and she loved him. I didn't want her to see me mistreating him the way he had done me. Therefore, I made up my mind that I was leaving once he recovered. I committed to staying until he could care for himself – three years….

Life Be Lifing (Pt. 1)

The Benediction

Finally, the moment I had been waiting for. Carrie was seven, about to turn eight, and our departure time was at hand. However, Mr. Gerard was in one of his nasty moods and had the nerve to tell our daughter, "Your mother is leaving because she wants to go turn tricks." Naturally, this made my baby cry, not knowing what it meant, but it was how he said it.

I stroked her hair as I said, "Do not cry; Daddy is just playing. Get in the car, okay?"

I said this because I did not want her to lose respect for him.

She walked out of the house. I looked at him and said, "If you knew who you were married to, you would never have said that. After what you did and what you have put me through and are still putting me through, you have the audacity to make a statement like that to your daughter, to my daughter. How dare you make an accusation like that about me?"

And once more, I must share Psalm 55:12-14: **12 For** *it is not an enemy* **who reproaches and taunts me—then I might bear it;** *nor is it one who has hated me* **who insolently vaunts himself against me—then I might hide from him. 13** *But it was you, a man my equal, my companion and my familiar friend.* **14We had** *sweet fellowship together and used to walk to the house of God in company* **(Psalm 55:12-14).**

Need I say more? And just like that, my time was up, and I walked out.

Sometimes, relationships cannot be mended, not because God cannot, but because He won't for His reasons. The key is recognizing the time and leaving with your head held high.

What the Devil Meant for Evil

I wasted no time in starting the divorce proceedings. Once again, Gerard didn't like what he could not control, so he made one last feeble attempt that didn't work.

Let me tell you: when you walk in the way of the Lord, the enemy will forge tools to work against you. But the Lord said in Isaiah 54:16-17 that those tools (weapons) wouldn't work!

While taking care of him, I took him to the Social Security office to apply for Social Security Disability Insurance (SSDI), which meant Carrie would also receive a check. I used this check to pay for her private school, piano lessons, and things of that nature. Naturally, the check was set up under my bank account, which did not sit well with Gerard. In his need for control, even from a sick bed, he went behind my back. All of a sudden, Carrie's deposits stopped

Life Be Lifing (Pt. 1)

coming. I did not get anxious about it because I know things can derail from time to time, so I waited a couple of days and still had no deposit. Then came another boom! Out of the blue, Gerard asks me, "Tammy, how much are Carrie's piano lessons?"

Hold the phone! Wait a minute right here. He's never asked about her lessons before. The lights came on, and I knew where this was going.

"So, Gerard, this wouldn't have anything to do with Carrie's deposit stopping suddenly, would it? You scandalous negro, did you have those deposits transferred? Don't you have enough misery going on without tampering with your child's well-being?"

He knew there was no way out except for the truth, as he muttered another "Yes" of guilt.

I was dumbfounded because I couldn't believe that I was running to and fro,' here and yonder, trying to take care of him, and he'd chosen to go behind my back to rob his child.

He'd done some nasty things to me, but I never thought he'd stoop so low to rattle his daughter's life or take revenge because he knew eventually, I would leave.

Well, tit, here comes tat, because now it's my turn. So, I called the Social Security office, and the man I spoke to was sent straight from God. He explained that Gerard had rerouted the check to his account, but it would be straightened out and the check would be sent to the right place; he placed a block so this could never happen again.

Chapter 6

LIFE BE LIFING - (PT. 2)

In 2008, Grandma Ruby, the woman who raised me, my grandmother, passed away. It was really difficult for me. Grandma Ruby was our family's rock, our matriarch. During this time, I had already moved out of the house from my husband and started divorce proceedings.

I got the call that my Grandma Ruby was not doing well and was in hospice. As you can imagine, I was already dealing with all of the issues with my husband, and now I'm losing my grandmother, the woman who raised me for the majority of my life.

She was the family's lifeline. She cooked Sunday weekly and taught us how to cook, clean, sew, etc. Grandma Ruby prepared us for life.

I didn't hesitate to fly back to Niagara Falls to see her one last time. She was in hospice at home, and Momma and Aunt Lynn were there when I walked into her room. I bent down and kissed her on the forehead as I sat down beside her.

Aunt Lynn said, "Hey, Mom, do you know who that is that kissed you?"

And with her last breath, Grandma softly answered, "It's my Baby."

She called me Baby. I never heard Tammy come out of her mouth. This beautiful, darling woman always had time for me, even if she didn't have an answer, and loved me unconditionally. Grandma made herself available.

I was holding her head as she took her final breath, and I heard someone say, "Tammy, she carried you all through your life, and now you've carried her into the next life."

This precious moment has been bookmarked in my heart for life. But a few days later, I would be faced with more drama.

I Feel Like David

Do you remember how King Saul chased David in 1 Samuel 21-24 in an effort to take his life? This is how I felt with Gerard pursuing me on every end, hoping to once more exercise control over my life.

My daughter was about eight years old during this time, and after returning to Atlanta from the funeral, I was served with papers; he was suing me for full custody of Carrie.

Life Be Lifing (Pt. 2)

For those who are married or have been married, we trust that our husbands have our best interests at heart. He is the covering for the home because God made him the head. Sadly, I never felt that covering. I suffered a lot under his domination, but I continued to hold my head up. Was it hard? Absolutely!

I had hoped my stern warning would have steered him away from this process, but he was determined to take me down. I was confident in how this would go; after all, look at his recent record... And so, after telling him, "You will never get full custody of my daughter. You will have to prove me an unfit mother, and that's not gonna happen. But if it's a fight you want, it's a fight you'll get."

During the mediation on visitation, I reassured Gerard that he could see Carrie whenever he wanted since she was his child as well. Despite the difficulties between Gerard and me, I was determined not to use our child as a tool for punishment. I made sure to keep her out of our conflicts because she was the most important thing.

Let this be a lesson to others: don't burden your child with your conflicts, and never make them choose sides. It's important to remember that your child's connection with their father doesn't end with a divorce, so it's crucial not to speak ill of the other parent because of the pain they may have caused you. Always take the high road.

It's also important that children aren't encouraged to speak against their father. As a person of faith, I believe in the commandment to "Honor thy father and thy mother that thy days may be long."[19]

So, the back-and-forth with the lawyers continued for a while until his mother told him to drop the lawsuit as she pressed hard the fact that a young girl needs to be with her mother.

We went to mediation. I couldn't keep the house because I wasn't making enough money to cover the mortgage, all the expenses, plus my daughter's private school, so I let the house go and moved into an apartment.

I'm thankful for a strong support team; my parents, my sisters, and close friends were always there to encourage me. My parents stepped in and helped me cover a lot of my bills for a while. My Dad, Pastor Grooms, made the ultimate sacrifice for me and Carrie. His weekly schedule included preaching at his church on Sunday mornings. He would then fly to us in Atlanta and stay with us through Thursday so that he could get Carrie up for school, drop her off, and pick her up because I had to be at work at 5:30 a.m. Dad and Momma both helped us out tremendously for almost a year. I'm so grateful to God for my Dad. This is another thing God did for me that I did not see coming.

Life Be Lifing (Pt. 2)

Because I never knew my seed father, God brought this wonderful man into my mom's life. This man has been more of a father to my sisters and me than you could imagine. I'm so grateful for him and my mother, Charlene, who has become my best friend.

Lifestyle Challenges

Carrie and I stayed in the apartment for about a year until a house became available for rent, and I moved us into a five-bedroom home for $1000 a month plus utilities. We lived there for a few years and then had to move because the homeowner was not paying the mortgage but used the money for her own personal gain.

It seemed to be a trend because, around that time, many renters were evicted because shady homeowners were renting their homes yet pocketing the money instead of paying the mortgage, leading to foreclosure.

Unfortunately, I was renting a home from a Vietnamese coworker, Thah Nguyen. When I asked about the mortgage payment due to the delinquent mortgage letters sent to the house, she claimed she was still making mortgage payments.

"Look," I said, "I want to see the last few months of statements proving that you've been paying the mortgage."

She could not comply, so I had to get another attorney to contact her. My lawyer advised her to present proof that she had been paying the mortgage, or she would be sued in court. She would be responsible for court fees and would have to return my deposit. Two days later, she sent me a check with the first and last month's rent plus deposit; I knew then that she had been doing something underhanded.

If the drama of the divorce and the crooked landlord wasn't enough, there was one more thing to add to my "to-do" list. Carrie and I needed a new place to live. A friend told me that her aunt was looking to rent her house. I went to see the nice one-level, three-bedroom house and quickly moved in. My daughter and I lived there for a few years; however, the landlady showed little interest in maintaining the property. Therefore, it was up to me to take on the added expense. In the meantime, a wrestling match was in full swing in my mind about this cycle of craziness in my life. But still, I was trying to stay focused and continue to lift my eyes unto the hills from which cometh my help.

Over time, things went well. I was able to pay my bills until things shifted again. Sometimes, my landlady would call me, crying. She wanted me to pray with her. I thought everything was good. You know, we were becoming friends, and then one day, out of the blue, she called in to say that she was selling the house. What?! I had 30 days to move out and found myself in the same situation again; it was heartbreaking. It was tough; I felt less of a mother because I seemed to have no stability for my daughter.

I had just filed for bankruptcy a couple of years prior because it was too much for me. I was stressed, gaining weight, and angry all the time until finally, I had enough.

Home-Sweet-Home

Philippians 4:6 encourages us, **"Do not be anxious about anything, but in everything by prayer and supplication with thanksgiving let your requests be made known to God."**

"Lord, I do not want to rent anymore. I want my own home." At this time, I was about to turn 50. It had been almost 50 years of hard life lessons.

I love my friends and family and how they celebrate everything. We celebrate holidays, anniversaries, birthdays, new jobs, new homes, etc. (LOL). But at this point in my life, I felt I had little to celebrate, especially my birthday.

I'm thankful for my family and their celebratory spirit, with the lavish parties, but in that season, a party wasn't my desire. However, my petition to the Father was to put my daughter in a home that belonged to us. A house that freed me from worry about anyone sending me an email or calling about renting a home, the landlord pocketing the rent money, or not maintaining the property.

After being subjected to foreclosure, it was time to hit the reset button in my life. My focus was on keeping a roof over our heads. Therefore, once again, I had to search for a new place for us. Finding another rental in a small community of starter homes didn't take long. It was a small three-bedroom upstairs and downstairs, but it was doable. I was grateful, but I wanted and deserved more. So, I told God I would live there for one year.

I began my search for a home and gave my realtor my wish list of what I would like in my home. Things were looking up for my credit because my bankruptcy had been discharged for about two years. I found a broker and gave them my information so they could start the process.

Financially, I felt pretty blessed as I made more money on my job. So, my realtor and I searched and searched, and the Lord blessed me with the ability to have my home built from the ground up. When I saw the model home, I fell in love with the floor plan.

It was a brand-new development that I learned about from Carrie.

"Mom, why don't you buy a house in Bristol Park?

"Bristol Park? I asked.

Life Be Lifing (Pt. 2)

"Yes, a lot of my friends at school live there."

We drove there, and as I pulled up, I saw these big, beautiful brick homes with gorgeous golf courses, tennis courts, and swimming pools. The property was simply stunning.

I looked at Carrie, "How much money do you think I make?"

She answered, "Mom, you can get one of these homes. Just pick one out."

Kids have no concept of money and bills, and I had also forgotten who I was talking to. This was the same little girl who, at three years of age, placed her dolls in a row and led them in worship service.

When I was searching for a place to stay a year earlier, I came across this property, but somehow, it had slipped my mind. I recall my realtor sending me listings of different models, but at that time, I didn't see the concept I wanted, but God had a plan!

House hunting took a huge turn one Saturday; while sitting quietly, the Lord said, "Get up and go for a ride."

As I drove around, He led me back to Bristol Park, where they had an open house. I entered the model house and immediately fell in love with the kitchen. It was huge.

From Pain to Purpose

The island was long and wide, with beautiful hardwood floors. It was the open concept I desired, and this was only the downstairs.

Standing in the kitchen, I said, "Lord, this must be my home."

Excited, I went upstairs to see the bedrooms, which turned out to be exactly what I envisioned. Huge bedrooms were on my list, and here they were.

I went home and prayed to the Lord about the house. I then called Dad, who flew in to see it. We looked at several models and eventually went to my favorite when he said, "This is your house right here."

Seeing the hand God move in my life so many times before, I wasn't surprised that Dad knew.

So, I talked with the agent, and she quoted me the price. We completed the necessary paperwork, and the agent showed me a map with my parcel of land where my house would be built. Look at God!

Happy Birthday to me! What a birthday present. I was speechless, tongue-tied, just plain unable to speak. There were no words for this moment.

I was 49 years old, and this would be my first solo homeowner experience. Before marriage, I lived with my grandparents. I'll never forget. It was March 2016, and Lord willing, I would see my 50th birthday in November. I began to really seek God about the house.

Before the building process, Dad flew in again with his anointing oil in hand. We poured oil over the land and then prayed over it.

I cannot describe the feeling of watching your house being built from the ground. I have never been more grateful and thankful for what God was doing. Everything moved so swiftly. That particular year, our pastor always gave a theme for the year during the New Year's Eve service, and that year, the theme was "Sweatless Victory."

Everything moved so well that I thought something was going to happen. I was looking for the proverbial other shoe to drop, to take it all away because it was moving so fast.

I picked out my land, and they gave me my new address. I watched my house go up. The Lord blessed me more than I could've ever imagined. When He said that He would open the window of heaven and pour out a blessing you won't have room enough to receive. He did it!

God blessed me with a 4000-plus-foot home with six bedrooms, a patio with a fireplace in the back, on a golf course community. I am so thankful to Him every day.

I turned 50 on November 3, 2016, and I closed my house on December 29th of the same year. God is faithful. I stayed in the atmosphere of praise because He inhabits our praise, and I needed Him near.

When I went to the closing, my father accompanied me. As we sat in the attorney's office, we looked at the couples who were also there to close on their new homes. For a short moment, I felt a little sad.

"Dad, look at all these couples here sharing this wonderful moment together, and I am alone."

Dad did what he do best. "Baby, you shouldn't feel that way. Look how God has blessed you as a single woman to do alone, what it normally takes two to accomplish. Be thankful, and be proud of what God is doing in your life."

Well, that powerful statement shut me up quickly. I've since learned to be content and keep a thankful heart in whatever state I am in.

I moved into my home on the same day, and every morning I get up, I tell God, "Thank You."

The first thing I did was create a War Room out of one of the spare bedroom closets. To those who don't know, a War Room dedicated to God where you can pray, read the

Bible, and meditate on God's Word. To this day, nothing is in the closet, but this is where I study, pray, and talk to the Lord. My daughter uses the room to pray and do her homework.

As I share my testimony, I pray it encourages someone's heart who has walked a similar path. Please know that if He did it for me, He will do the same for you. God will never leave you nor forsake you. There is a way out!

Even through my heartache and pain, I didn't know that my life had a purpose. The enemy would make us think that there is no plan or reason for being here on Earth, and so we forsake our relationship with God. We're told in Romans 8:16-18 that the Spirit of God sealed us as the children of God when we accepted Christ. Since we are His children, we became joint heirs with Christ; if we are willing to suffer with Him by bearing our crosses, we may also be glorified together. So, the light afflictions and the suffering I had to endure don't compare to what's ahead for me.

In the midst of the suffering, we are also encouraged in 3 John 1:2: **"Beloved, I wish above all things that thou mayest prosper and be in health even as your soul prospers."** We must stand on God's Word and trust that even though things don't work out the way we would like, He has a plan that will work. The plans of God cannot be compared to anything else. Proverbs 3:5 says to "Trust in Him with all your heart and lean not on your own understanding. In all our ways, acknowledge him, and He will direct your path."

Chapter 7

SEE WHAT THE LORD HAS DONE

I moved out and got my own apartment as I pressed forward to do things for myself and my daughter. It was tough, but in time things got better.

Carrie and I continued to get tested for HIV twice a year until, after several years, my doctor told me it was no longer needed and that neither of us had HIV. To God be the glory! I shudder to think how a positive result would have altered her life. I know God would have been there for her, but as a mother, I didn't want that for my daughter.

Romans 8:28 says, **"And we know that all things work together for good to them that love God, and are called according to his purpose."**

I pondered the scripture for a while, wondering what good could come from a broken marriage and how my ex-husband brought others and disease into our home.

So, I began to question God.

"How is this working for my good?"

I cried almost every night, wondering why my husband was so distant.

"Was that working together for my good?"

Taking my daughter and myself to get tested every six months.

"Lord, was that working for my good?"

Having to live with a man who treated me badly and then stayed and prepared his meals and medicines."

"Father, God, was that working for my good?"

I took him to his infectious disease doctor and sat with him.

"Please tell me, Lord, how was this working for my good?

I questioned everything about me, my existence, and my salvation.

"How is all this hurt, pain, and humiliation working together for my good?"

"God, why did I have to go through this? Do you know how humiliating and how hurtful it was to hold onto this secret and not be able to say anything because I felt embarrassed?"

Whenever our relationships go bad, we women always internalize by asking what is wrong with us. I did it as I questioned everything about myself. Why doesn't he love me? Am I not good enough? But I tried to stay encouraged as best I could. And then, I redirected the questions to the Father...

Y'all know God is not afraid of any of us, and my questions didn't cause Him to flinch. He allowed me the time to tell him about my feelings, how my heart was broken, and how I was disappointed in the way things turned out. And then, in His time, He answered me.

One Sunday, while working from home and watching my church service, my Pastor was preaching on "Trusting in the Midst of the Storm." He quoted Romans 8:28, and something shifted in me when I heard the voice of God say, "Daughter, I had to allow you to go through this test. I watched the countless nights you cried, feeling that you were alone. I smiled as I watched you create and plan the couple's getaways and how he refused. I listened to the negative self-talk, the many times you felt like you were not good enough and felt abandoned in the marriage, all while he chipped away at your self-esteem. I saw that you slept in separate rooms and how that affected you. If you had not gone through that, My child, and gotten what you desired from this marriage, you would have a different story today.

Although it didn't feel like it, I covered you, and so your testimony is that of a woman and her child who are HIV-negative!

There is POWER in the blood; I believe Jesus's blood cleansed, purified, and protected both me and my daughter.

She's thriving, doing very well in college, majoring in marketing, and has pledged to Delta Sigma Theta with future entrepreneurial plans. I'm thriving as well, and now I know my purpose. I had to go through that so I could be here to encourage someone else. When He said all things work together for good, He didn't say that all things were good; however, they did aid in our good outcome.

Sometimes, things happen that you don't understand, but it's for a reason and a purpose. Some things we go through can hurt our very soul and make us question everything about ourselves, down to our very existence.

During difficult times, it's common for fear to take hold, causing us to lose focus on seeking solutions. Instead of fixating on the problem, we should shift our focus to the problem solver. While this may be easier said than done, in the end, it proves to be beneficial. It's important to remember that God, in His mercy, witnesses and understands all that we endure. The Bible says, **Consider it pure joy, my brothers and sisters, whenever you face trials of many kinds, ³because you know that the testing of your faith produces perseverance.**

⁴**Let perseverance finish its work so that you may be mature and complete, not lacking anything."**[20]

From this day forward, I have decided to embrace the journey ahead. It is time for me to draw upon all my past experiences and channel them towards fulfilling God's purpose in my life. I am committed to sharing my personal narrative through this book, public speaking engagements, and everyday interactions. I want to convey to others that life presents its share of challenges. Our faith does not exempt us from the trials and tribulations of life. Often, we find ourselves grappling with uncertainties, resorting to a "fake it till you make it" mentality as we navigate through life's complexities. Too much time and effort are spent attempting to decipher our path, followed by further pondering on whether our choices will yield the desired outcome. We truly lack a deep understanding of what is revealed in the Word.

David, the great king of Israel, made an observation regarding this very issue. He spoke of his community's moral and social chaos by divine inspiration and described the root cause of humanity's confusion, frustration, and self-destruction. They know nothing; they understand nothing; they walk about in darkness, and the foundation of the Earth is shaking sounds (Psalm 82).

The challenges and confusion faced by people on Earth are not due to a lack of answers but rather stem from our limited understanding of our Creator. Our lack of knowledge about His principles, purpose, nature, and precepts has contributed to the numerous issues we encounter. Ignorance of oneself is the greatest adversary of humanity. There is nothing more perplexing than not comprehending your identity or how to utilize your potential. The problems experienced by people can be traced back to this fundamental quandary. Essentially, our lack of understanding leads to a life filled with uncertainty, and frustration becomes the inevitable outcome. Obtaining insight into God's ways can transform your spirit, mind, and overall perspective. It's essential to recognize that each individual is greatly cherished by God, as evidenced by the sacrifice of His only Son for the human race.

God has placed something unique in each one of us and, therefore, desires our salvation so that we can fulfill the purpose for which He gave us life. We need to seek him earnestly to discover that purpose. [21]

The Residue of Repeated Behavior

In recent years, I've realized that life has improved significantly, and my vision has become clearer since I discovered my purpose. Through the highs and lows of various relationships, breakups, and heartaches, I've learned much about myself. It wasn't until my most recent relationship ended abruptly that I finally acknowledged the self-hate that had been plaguing me all along, leaving me in a place I never wished to return to.

I'm being very transparent now, so please don't judge; pray for me because we all have our different moments of spiritual clarity.

I devoted everything to this man – my love, body, and heart. But it felt like I was back in my marriage, where any disagreement would lead to him getting angry and storming off or where asking too many questions would result in him calling me names. I did my best to keep him happy, but I felt neglected. I convinced myself that as long as he was happy, everything was okay, even though deep down, I was miserable. I had to put on a happy face so I wouldn't have to face my loneliness.

I was taken advantage of in many ways in my relationships, thinking because we had so much in common: our upbringing in the church and the same taste in music; he was a drummer, which has always been one of my instruments of choice. We talked all the time. He became my best friend, and it was nice to finally have someone truly interested in me. He took time out to talk about my likes and dislikes, and he shared his with me; we both shared stories about our childhood and adolescence stages.

I did more in this relationship than in my marriage, so I grew closer to this guy. He met my family, we met each other's children, and everything was great. I thought I had finally met "the one." This went on for a few years, and in hindsight, I should have recognized some flags, but when we get in our feelings, we ignore them. But more than that, I didn't consult the Father.

We women sometimes ignore the red flags that are slapping us in the face, thinking that if we love them enough, a change will take place. Yeah, right. We must understand that we do not have the power or authority to change anyone.

However, the reality of our relationship was bookmarked in my heart after he talked to my parents and told them of his desire to marry me. Yay me! But just as quickly, a few weeks later, he had the audacity to turn around to say that he just wanted to be friends and that marriage was not in our future after all those years of playing house and acting like we were working toward something permanent. Needless to say, I was crushed and humiliated. Why? Because I fell for the okie-doke. I didn't use discernment or notes from my failed marriage. I can't lie; I was so hurt that I couldn't breathe. I cried until I couldn't.

What Happens in the War Room

Again, I felt this sense of worthlessness, and my self-esteem chipped away AGAIN. Why was I repeating this cycle? What was going on within me that kept me attracting the same type of man? I needed answers.

After about a week of this thought process, I went into my War Room and cried out to God. Time and pages don't allow me to share every detail because what is shared in the War Room stays in the War Room, but the changes are manifested outside of the War Room.

"Lord, please mend my broken heart. I want to take our relationship to another level. I need your strength to get through this healing process and to kill the root of the issue that keeps me in this repeat cycle of bad relationship choices. Thank You, in the name of Jesus. Amen."

Did it happen overnight? Of course not. That would have been a miracle, and Father wanted me to do some work on myself. Philippians 2:2 tells us, **"Therefore, my beloved, as ye have always obeyed, not only in my presence, but now much more in my absence, work out your own salvation with fear and trembling."**

This does not refer to our soul's salvation. This is the work we have to do to get rid of the root of the cycle of bad decisions, old wounds, and trauma we tend to ignore and cover up with shopping, overeating, drinking, drugs, and sex. It's working on those harmful habits we can't seem to quit, as well as bad attitudes and thoughts. This soul work takes time, and we don't allow God the time to help us because there is suffering involved, and we don't give others time for their process because we keep expecting miracles where work is supposed to be.

I continued to pray, and each time I thought about what he had done, I wanted to cry from the gut-wrenching pain, I took it to God in prayer.

People of God, I don't remember when it happened, but He delivered me. I found that I could sleep peacefully again. I smiled as I discovered the old flame had died out, and the ex-lover was no longer taking up free space in my mind or heart. God did an excellent job of erasing him! To God be the Glory!

This encouraged me to start seriously working on myself; I asked God to help me see myself through His eyes. Now, I know that sounds good, but when the truth of who we are and what really needs work is revealed, it can be shocking and painful.

Now, I'm not saying that God is looking down His nose at us. But everything about us is not ice cream and cake either! However, what I recognized when I made this statement was that God was calling me to do deeper things that I was now ready for.

Purpose

Purpose, defined, is *the reason something is done, created, or exists*. Believers often spend a great deal of time searching for purpose, not knowing that every season of life serves its own purpose.

God never intended for us to find one thing and focus on that. But has created an individual script for each of us to follow as we go through and grow through the seasons of our lives. Therefore, I was shaped by trials of fire through the University of Adversity so that I could serve this present season to minister to women and men who have a similar life experience and to help the younger people not to fall into a similar trap.

Purpose does not come in pretty gift wrapping. No. Purpose comes after several beat downs by life, and you find yourself standing strong, being held by the powerful right hand of God! Purpose puts you to work in the area where you have experienced spiritual growth from those very long times of suffering. So yes, I can say I have more than one purpose.

God said it best in the Word. Those of us who have gone through and are now equipped for purpose graduated as He appoint(s) unto them that mourn in Zion, to give unto them beauty for ashes, the oil of joy for mourning, the garment of praise for the spirit of heaviness, that they might be called trees of righteousness, the planting of the Lord, that He might be glorified (Isaiah 61:3)."

Purpose revealed means it's time to work. As the Scripture says, God has chosen us to assist those who come behind us in transforming from the darkness of ignorance to the light of knowledge in Christ Jesus. We become ambassadors for Christ in the gospel message.

Beauty for Ashes

One day, I was at home in my office working, listening to gospel music, when the song "Endow Me" by the Clark sisters came on. A change began to take place as I absorbed the words of this song into my spirit: *"To lay hands and to discern. To understand God's holy Word. To speak in tongues and give interpretations. To prophesy with edification. Move in the midst of thy people. Move in me, Lord, like Shekinah Glory from on high."*[22]

First, I started crying and thanking God; however, as the words continued to speak to me, the Holy Spirit made His presence known.

That was it! I began praising God so much I couldn't stop. I got up, walked into the room next to my office, and bent over in worship. The Holy Spirit was on me so heavily that I could not stand straight up. I don't know how long I was in that room; frankly, I didn't care. I felt something I hadn't felt in a long time. I had forgotten the feeling of God's presence. It was like Jeremiah said. It felt like fire shut up in my bones.

Yeah, I know, I've heard it plenty of times because we have completely modernized God, and so it's believed that "It doesn't take all of that," and that is what the enemy wants us to think. I'm here to tell you it takes that and then some! God said He is the same yesterday, today, and forever.

I made that U-turn back to Christ, and I feel so blessed now in my walk with Him because I know He did something in me that day; I have not been the same since.

I am so in love with my heavenly father that I'm in tears as I write these words to you. All these years, I have been searching for true, true love, wondering all my adult life if I will ever experience what real unconditional love is. I did not realize that I already had the greatest love of my life all this time, and His name is Jesus!

We will never have anyone in our lives who will love us as He does. I am beyond blessed as I discover how much He loves me. I no longer wonder about the lack of successful relationships in my life. I don't ruminate over my ex-husband finding someone and remarrying. I am thankful that Father God did not allow me to marry again, and I'll tell you why. After all of the things I have gone through and God brought me through, I no longer wonder about anything in my future because I know who holds it. I have since learned my worth and how to love myself. I can finally look in the mirror and love the woman looking back at me.

I didn't know I was not loving myself for so many years. I had allowed people to beat me down to the point that I would only look in the mirror to put on mascara, and I didn't like my body shape. I did not realize that I was the prize, that I was fearfully and wonderfully made by God for His purpose.[23] Therefore, I actually apologized to myself for the years of abuse and accepted the way I allowed people to treat me and speak to me. I apologized to myself for the times I kept my mouth shut when I should have spoken up. Instead, I convinced myself there was nothing to defend. I apologized for buying into the lie that I don't have a testimony and, most of all, for making myself feel unloved.

Now, I have been blessed to have many doors opening for me. I promised God that when 2024 came in, this would be the year of dreams coming true for me and my family. I asked Him for favor and began to thank Him in advance for the doors He was opening doors of opportunities I didn't know I wanted.

See What the Lord Has Done

In the middle of 2023, God put me on a weight loss journey. Now, I do not know why He did it, but nevertheless, at His word. Since then, with no surgeries, I lost a total of 79 lbs. I'm blessed to be able to work out at the gym every weekday morning at 4 am. I implemented swimming in my workout, dancing, and walking 5 miles per day on my off day.

I'm now being approached by people inquiring if I'm a model, and when they discover I'm not. I've been told to consider it.

I've been invited to photo shoots, and I get people calling me to model in their fashion shows every day. Now, remember, I am the same person who was called Olive Oil, who had short hair and was socially inept for a while. But see what the Lord has done. He has exchanged my ashes for beauty! Lord, I just want to thank You for trusting in me to do Your will and fulfill Your purpose for my life!

Amen and Amen!

Final Thoughts

The true evidence of my change is through my daughter, Carrie. I've made it a point to speak life into her from the womb that she was a leader. She is almost 24 years old today, and I am so godly proud of her.

As I stated earlier, she has had her tests and challenges as well, some similar to mine. Where my loved ones failed me, because of my "go-through" and victorious coming out, I can provide her with some positive directions.

Carrie has greatly excelled in her short 24 years on earth. Some so-called "friends" were pouring gallons of hate-o-rade, but I pointed out that these people were not for her. God had plans that didn't include them, so He was trying to redirect her path from them so she wouldn't get distracted.

I know God's hand is in and through her life, so I must share some of the goodness. She was the president of the NAACP in college, had the opportunity to speak with President Biden on Zoom, worked with Senators John Ossoff and Raphael Warnock, and has traveled extensively out of the country.

Carrie is active in community affairs, various auxiliaries, and positions on campus and has represented her college on two occasions in Virginia.

Again, with God's direction, I've intentionally prepared her heart and mind to live a life for Christ and to exude His love for everyone she meets. My daughter is ready! So much more than I was at her age. Thank You, Father, for the "go through" of the University of Adversity so that I could help Carrie better maneuver through life. So, when we talk about Purpose, you can't leave out legacy; they go hand in hand.

Thank you for your time and patience as I wrap up my narrative. I pray you embrace longsuffering as a good soldier, learn from it, grow from it, and use it to help someone else as you are established in your own purpose.

Blessings to you,

Tammy

About the Author

The esteemed author of this captivating book, Tammy Renee, epitomizes a rare blend of unwavering commitment, remarkable drive, and impeccable character. At the core of her being lies a profound love for Christ, the foundation for her life's work and writing. Tammy's faith imbues her words with deep spiritual insight and compassion, offering readers a transformative journey through the power of her storytelling.

Beyond her literary endeavors, Tammy's devotion to her family shines brightly. Her love for her daughter is palpable in every facet of her life, from the tender moments shared to the guidance imparted with unwavering support. As a mother, Tammy embodies strength and grace, nurturing her family with a selfless dedication that reflects her values and faith. Her commitment to her craft and loved ones paints a portrait of resilience and compassion, demonstrating how her faith and family intertwine to shape a life filled with purpose and love. Tammy Renee's story is not just one of literary achievement but of a profound journey marked by faith, family, and the enduring power of love.

For more information about this author:

@tammyrenee

Tammyrenee2357@gmail.com

Endnotes

[1] King James Version (KJV) - Version information - BibleGateway.com. (n.d.). https://www.biblegateway.com/versions/King-James-Version-KJV-Bible/

Introduction

[2] Psalms 91:5-6, 5Thou shalt not be afraid for the terror by night; nor for the arrow that flieth by day; 6 Nor for the pestilence that walketh in darkness; nor for the destruction that wasteth at noonday.

[3] Psalm 139:14, 14 I will praise thee; for I am fearfully and wonderfully made: marvellous are thy works; and that my soul knoweth right well.

[4] Jeremiah 29:11, For I know the thoughts that I think toward you, saith the Lord, thoughts of peace, and not of evil, to give you an expected end.

Chapter 1 – Who Am I?

[5] The name has been changed to Ruby to protect the privacy of the individual.

[6] The name has been changed to Jim to protect the privacy of the individual.

Chapter 2 – Life with Mom

[7] Psalm 27:10 - Create in me a clean heart, O God; And renew a right spirit within me. Cast me not away from thy presence; And take not thy holy spirit from me. Restore unto me the joy of thy salvation; And uphold me with thy free spirit.

[8] The name has been changed to Ms. Lamar to protect the privacy of the individual.

[9] The name was changed to Mrs. Dunphy to protect the privacy of the individual.

Chapter 3 – There's No Place Like Home

[10] The name has been changed to Principal Jones to protect the privacy of the individual

Chapter 4 – Who Did I Marry?

[11] The name has been changed to Sandra to protect the privacy of the individual

[12] The name has been changed to Walter Grooms to protect the privacy of the individual.

[13] Ruby Redfort quotes. (n.d.). https://www.goodreads.com/author/quotes/15285269.Ruby_Redfort

[14] The name has been changed to Ms. Gladys to protect the privacy of the individual

Chapter 5 – Life Be Lifing (Pt. 1)

[15] The name has been changed to Dr. Lansing to protect the privacy of the individual.

[16] The name has been changed to Jake to protect the privacy of the individual

[17] Almost 5 million new AIDS cases in 2005. (2005, November 21). NBC News. https://www.nbcnews.com/id/wbna10137632

[18] The Diary of a Mad Black Woman. Tyler Perry. (2005).

Chapter 6 – Life Be Lifing (Pt. 2)

[19] Exodus 20:12, Honour thy father and thy mother: that thy days may be long upon the land which the LORD thy God giveth thee.

Chapter 7 – See What the Lord Has Done

[20] James 1:2 (NIV) - Consider it pure joy, my brothers and sisters,[a] whenever you face trials of many kinds, 3 because you know that the testing of your faith produces perseverance. 4 Let perseverance finish its work so that you may be mature and complete, not lacking anything."

[21] Jacque St. Jude Johnson Sr. (2022, December 1). Dr. Myles Munroe | The Greatest Enemy of Man Is Ignorance [Video]. YouTube. https://www.youtube.com/watch?v=u3sMRsWHUaw

[22] Clark Sisters. (2024, May 26). You Brought the Sunshine. In Wikipedia. https://en.wikipedia.org/wiki/You_Brought_the_Sunshine

[23] Psalm 139: 14 - I will praise thee; for I am fearfully and wonderfully made: marvelous are thy works; and that my soul knoweth right well.

Made in the USA
Columbia, SC
26 October 2024